AF505079

The Workings
of Memory

The Workings of Memory

Life-Writing by Women in Early Twentieth-Century Spain

Sarah Leggott

Lewisburg
Bucknell University Press

Associated University Presses
2010 Eastpark Boulevard
Cranbury, NJ 08512

The paper used in this publication meets the requirements of the America National Standard for Permanence of Paper for Printed Library Materials Z39.48-1984.

Library of Congress Cataloging-in-Publication Data

Leggott, Sarah.
The Workings of memory : life-writing by women in early twentieth-century Spain / Sarah Leggott.
    p. cm.
Includes bibliographical references and index.
ISBN 978-0-8387-5682-9 (alk. paper)
1. Spanish literature—Women authors—History and criticism. 2. Spanish literature—20th century—History and criticism. 3. Women and literature—Spain. 4. Women in literature. 5. Autobiography in literature. 1. Title.
PQ6055.L437   2008
860.9′9287—dc22
                                      2007025326

To Stuart

Contents

Acknowledgments

I RECEIVED IMPORTANT FUNDING FOR THIS STUDY FROM THE MARSDEN Fund of the Royal Society of New Zealand, as well as research grants from both the Faculty of Humanities and Social Sciences Research Committee and the University Research Fund at Victoria University of Wellington. I am very grateful for this financial support of my research.

My sincere thanks are due to Christine Arkinstall, both for her enthusiasm for my project and for her insightful critique of many drafts. Her feedback was invaluable for helping me to develop and refine my ideas. I also thank Wendy-Llyn Zaza for her encouragement and for her generous help with challenging translations. My thanks go also to the research assistants who contributed to this project: Karen McLellan, José Díaz, Kushla Beacon, and Gwyn Fox, and to my colleagues in the School of Asian and European Languages and Cultures at Victoria University of Wellington for their support.

In Spain, I thank Miguel Ángel Arnedo and Ana Isabel Gómez for their friendship and help, as well as for a truly memorable visit to La Rioja. Thanks also to friends in Madrid, especially Segis and Marisol, David, Estela, Ana, and Guille, for their company during various research trips.

The completion of this project would not have been possible without the continued support, encouragement, and love of my immediate family; my thanks go particularly to my parents, Ailsa and Michael, and, as always, to Stuart. Stuart, Ryan, and now Lauren, have accompanied me on some busy, but always exciting, research trips to Spain, and their company and support there were invaluable.

Finally, my thanks go to Professor Greg Clingham of Bucknell University Press and to the production team at Associated University Presses.

Some of the material included in chapters four and five has previously appeared in articles published in the *Hispanic Journal* (USA).

I am grateful to the editors of this journal for permission to reprint this material.

In addition, an article currently in press in *AUMLA* (Journal of the Australasian Universities Language and Literature Association) contains material on the Lyceum Club that is reproduced in this study.

The Workings
of Memory

Introduction: Women on the Literary Scene in Early Twentieth-Century Madrid

THIS STUDY FOCUSES ON THE LIFE-WRITING PRODUCED BY FOUR WOMEN writers and intellectuals of early twentieth-century Spain: Carmen Baroja (1883–1950), María Martínez Sierra (1874–1974), María Teresa León (1903–1988), and Concha Méndez (1898–1986).[1] Active in the cultural arena in early twentieth-century Madrid, albeit in different ways and to varying degrees, Baroja, Martínez Sierra, León, and Méndez, like so many of their contemporaries, were all relegated to critical oblivion following the Spanish Civil War. It is the autobiographical narratives produced by these four writers that form the basis of this study.

The exclusion of women writers from the annals of Spanish literary history has been well documented by critics and historians, and much work has been done over recent decades to inscribe women into both the historical and the literary records, particularly in the field of twentieth-century literature. However, despite the significant progress that has been made in this area, the majority of studies of twentieth-century Spanish women writers focus on authors of the post–Civil War and post-Franco periods, with women writing in the first decades of the century receiving considerably less critical attention. This absence is confirmed by Teresa Bordons, who refers to the "hiatus of silence" (1993, 2) surrounding women who wrote between the end of the nineteenth century and the postwar period.[2]

The decades that constitute the focus of this study are often referred to as the *Edad de Plata,* or Silver Age, of Spanish literature and culture, indicating the esteem in which canonical writers of the period are held. Spanish literary history has traditionally referred to these writers as members of different literary "generations," with the best known of these the "Generation of 1898" and the "Generation of 1927." While the generational model has been called into question by critics, it nevertheless continues to be widely used to refer to literary production of the period in question. The exclusionary politics inherent in this model will be discussed in this study, with a particular focus on the positioning of women writers in regard to the generations from which they were excluded.[3]

Despite their systematic exclusion from the canon, research reveals the presence in early twentieth-century Spain of quite a number of women who were actively participating in cultural arenas traditionally reserved for men. Moreover, some of the women who were writing and publishing during this period received recognition and positive critical attention at that time. In fact, critic Gregory Cole affirms that "[t]he Generation of 1927 produced more published women poets and writers than any previous generation" (2000, 173).[4] Within this group are poets Josefina de la Torre, Ernestina de Champourcin, Concha Méndez, Elisabeth Mulder, Pilar de Valderrama, Carmen Conde, and Rosa Chacel. Outside the genre of poetry, other female literary figures of the period include María Martínez Sierra, María Zambrano, María Teresa León, Concha Espina, Carmen de Burgos, Margarita Nelken, Blanca de los Ríos, Sofía Casanova, and Federica Montseny. In addition, Emilia Pardo Bazán, a key figure in late nineteenth-century literature, was still writing during the first two decades of the twentieth century.[5]

These writers and intellectuals, whom Anna Caballé designates "the other Generation of 1927" (1998, 127), were all active in the literary scene of early twentieth-century Spain and were integrated, in varying degrees, in literary circles of the period. They had various publishing and personal ties with their male contemporaries, and they published their works in many of the same journals as their male peers. In addition to publishing in such outlets, a number of women were also involved in their production: this is, for example, the case of León who, with her husband, Rafael Alberti, set up the political publication *Octubre,* and of Méndez who, with her husband, Manuel Altolaguirre, published *El Caballo Verde para la Poesía, 1616,* and *Héroe.* Likewise, Martínez Sierra, together with her husband Gregorio and others, was involved in the publication of the Modernist journals *Helios* and *Renacimiento.*

Despite such activities and connections, women writers of the early twentieth century have all but disappeared from literary records. While it is true that some of these women do have more visibility than others, their public profile is generally not due to their literary accomplishments of the 1920s and 1930s. While Conde and Chacel, for example, are well-known writers, this is primarily due to their later publications. Conde is not normally included in discussions of poets of this era, due to the fact that most of her work was published in a later period. She was, however, writing and publishing in the 1920s and 1930s, with her first volume of poetry, entitled *Brocal* [The Well's Edge] appearing in 1929, followed by *Júbilos* [Rejoicings] in 1934 (Conde 1967). Similarly, Chacel was active as a poet in the early 1930s, publishing her first poems in literary magazines, followed by the publication of her volume of poetry, *A la orilla de un pozo* [At the Edge of a Well], in 1936. Although Chacel is without doubt recognized as a distinguished figure in Spanish literary history, she is best known for her novels and essays.

The personal relationships between women writers of this period and male literary figures is a further factor that has contributed to both their visibility and, paradoxically, their marginalization. Examples of such relationships include the marriages between León and Alberti, Méndez and Altolaguirre, María de la O Lejárraga (Martínez Sierra) and Gregorio Martínez Sierra, and Champourcin and Juan José Domenchina. The relationships that these women maintained with members of the male literary elite arguably resulted in their enjoying a greater integration into the literary scene than they might otherwise have achieved, providing them with opportunities to meet other writers and to join in a wide range of professional activities. Conversely, however, said relationships simultaneously further contributed to their marginalization, for they were seen only as the wives of poets and writers, rather than as literary figures in their own right, as John Wilcox has argued (1994, 292). This is certainly the case of León, who is more widely known for having been the wife of Alberti than for her own contribution to Spanish literature. While Baroja was not married to a writer or artist, her two brothers, Ricardo and Pío, were very much part of the cultural elite of Madrid at the turn of the century.

Carmen Baroja was, then, a member of one of Spain's most prominent literary families, yet she herself received little support from her relatives for her cultural endeavors in the areas of handcraft, metal and enamel work, and literature. It is her experiences as a woman in a family dominated by male writers and artists, and in a society that offered few opportunities for women in the cultural arena, that Baroja documents in her autobiography, *Recuerdos de una mujer de la generación del 98* [Memories of a Woman of the Generation of 1898] (1998). Written in the 1940s, Baroja's manuscript remained unpublished until 1998, when its unordered pages were compiled by Amparo Hurtado.

María de la O Lejárraga, better known by her married name of María Martínez Sierra, under which she published her two autobiographical texts, wrote numerous plays and essays from the turn of the century until the early 1930s, nearly all of which appeared under the name of her husband, Gregorio Martínez Sierra.[6] In addition to her literary activities, María Martínez Sierra was an important feminist political figure in Spain in the 1920s and 1930s: she held several important roles in the Socialist Party and was elected to Parliament in 1933. In her literary writings, essays, and political campaigns, it is the question of women's rights that is at the forefront of Martínez Sierra's concerns. Such concerns are likewise reflected in her autobiographical works, particularly in *Una mujer por caminos de España* [A Woman on the Roads of Spain] (1989), which was written in the 1930s and 1940s and first published in 1952. Her second autobiographical work, entitled *Gregorio y yo: Medio siglo de colaboración* [Gregorio and I: Half a Century of Collaboration] (2000), written in the 1940s and first published in 1953, focuses on the author's personal and literary life story.

María Teresa León, perhaps the best known of the four women included in this study, wrote her autobiography entitled *Memoria de la melancolía* [Memory of Melancholy] (1998) in the 1960s from exile in Italy. A prolific creative writer in a wide range of literary genres, León was also politically active as a member of the Communist Party during the years of the Republic and Civil War. León's autobiography details her experiences in Spain in the first decades of the twentieth century—from her childhood years to her political activism in the 1930s—and goes on to document the war years and her subsequent experience of exile in France, Argentina, and Italy.

The memoirs of poet Concha Méndez, entitled *Memorias habladas, memorias armadas* [Spoken Memories, Assembled Memories] (1990), are based on recordings made in the 1980s by Méndez's granddaughter, Paloma Ulacia Altolaguirre. It is Méndez's participation in the cultural and literary scene of Madrid in the 1920s and 1930s and, more specifically, her association with the male members of the "Generation of 1927" that her text seeks to document. Méndez published some ten volumes of poetry, as well as a number of plays, both in Spain between 1926 and 1939 and later in exile in Mexico. She was also involved in the publication of important literary journals of the period, in collaboration with her husband, Manuel Altolaguirre.

There are, of course, important differences among the four writers who form the basis of this study. The first and perhaps most obvious of these is the authors' birthdates, which span a twenty-year period, indicating that they experienced a somewhat different historical context: Baroja and Martínez Sierra lived their childhood and adolescence in the final decades of the nineteenth century, while León and Méndez grew up amidst the social changes and modernization of the early twentieth century. Such age differences are naturally reflected also in the years in which these women began writing and publishing. That women writers of early twentieth-century Spain fall into two distinct groupings, those who started publishing between 1898 and 1918 and those whose literary careers commenced between 1918 and 1936, is confirmed by Hurtado, who affirms that "whereas the second group belonged fully to the twentieth century, the initial group of women writers . . . was still evolving on the cusp of the two centuries, fluctuating between tradition and modernity" (1998a, 143). Hurtado includes Baroja and Martínez Sierra among the earlier writers, and León is mentioned as a member of the later group; while Hurtado does not mention Méndez, she would also fall among the "modern" writers of the early twentieth century.

Details of these four writers' literary careers and published works also serve to highlight their individuality—while León, for example, was a prolific writer with over twenty published literary works in a wide range of genres, Baroja published only two books, apart from her memoirs and a volume of poetry, both of which were published posthumously.[7] The forms of life-writing produced by these women and the dates of publication of these works are similarly diverse. While Baroja wrote her *Recuerdos de una mujer de la generación del 98* during the 1940s, it was first published in 1998, almost fifty years after the author's death. Martínez Sierra produced two accounts of her life: she started writing the first, *Una mujer por caminos de España*, in the 1930s, during a period in which the author was at the forefront of political activism; the second, *Gregorio y yo*, was written in the 1940s and first published in 1953. In contrast, León wrote her *Memoria de la melancolía*, which appeared in print in 1970, during the 1960s, from the perspective of the intellectual in exile. The interviews on which Méndez's *Memorias habladas, memorias habladas* is based were made in the early 1980s in the final years of the author's life, and the work was published in 1990. The relative proximity to or distance from the events recounted inevitably affects the representation of the past presented in these writers' works and has important implications for the workings of the memory process. The

narrative styles adopted by these four writers also vary: while Martínez Sierra's prose is quite clear and concise and Baroja adopts a con-
versational and somewhat self-critical style, León's writing is fluid
and poetic in nature. The oral nature of Méndez's memoirs inevitably results in a less formal, more colloquial account.

The women who form the basis of this study are also differently
positioned in terms of education, political involvement, levels of
family support for their endeavors, and financial resources, and it is,
of course, important to take into account such differences between
women who were active on the cultural scene. However, despite such
diversity, there nevertheless exist similarities and points of contact
among them also. Baroja, Martínez Sierra, León, and Méndez were
all based in Madrid; they all came from middle-class families; they
were, to varying degrees, in contact with each other and with other
women involved in the literary and cultural scene of the day; they all
had ties to male members of Madrid's literary elite; and their works
were published in some of the same literary publications. Taken together, and examined as a group, these autobiographical narratives
shed much light on the realities of life for the female intellectual in
early twentieth-century Spain.

While this period of Spanish cultural and literary history has received an increased amount of critical attention in recent years, the
focus of the present study sets it apart from other works. Recent
studies have discussed, for example, women poets and intellectuals
of the period in question, the involvement of women in the Modernist movement of the first decades of the twentieth century and questions of gender in novels of this period. In particular, Catherine
Bellver's work on Spanish women poets of the 1920s and 1930s
(2001), Susan Kirkpatrick's analysis of women's involvement in the
Modernist and avant-garde movements in Spain between 1898 and
1931 (2003), and Shirley Mangini's discussion of the women whom
she designates the "modernas de Madrid" [modern women of Ma-
drid] (2001) are all groundbreaking studies in this field and are
works to which this study is indebted.[8]

My own focus, however, is on the life-writing produced by Baroja,
Martínez Sierra, León, and Méndez. This book examines the ways in
which these writers, in their autobiographical narratives, portray
their positioning in relation to dominant cultural models of the
time, and considers the extent to which they engaged with or refused such discourses. In addition, the way in which these women
were positioned in relation to each other and to their male contem-

poraries is discussed, with a focus on the question of how their relationships with their male contemporaries in the literary world and with their families enabled or limited their cultural agency. This study also seeks to illuminate the ways in which these writers engaged with political and social issues in a period of changing gender dynamics and political instability, and the ways in which their gender inflected the production and reception of their works.

In broader terms, through its focus on the autobiographical narratives produced by Baroja, Martínez Sierra, León, and Méndez, this study examines the complex relationships between memory, writing, and identity, and thus contributes to the growing field of explorations of the workings of memory in narrative. These are issues that have been the focus of much recent scholarly interest and interdisciplinary debate, with the question of how the past enters and shapes representations in the present central to contemporary autobiographical discourses. Literary and cultural studies have explored the limits of the representation of the self and the problematic status of writing in the first person, particularly for women, revealing the ways in which the contested meanings ascribed to terms such as "self" and "subject" in current theoretical debate have served to problematize traditional notions of a coherent and unified autobiographical subject.[9] The supposed authenticity of narrative accounts of life stories has been called into question by theorists, with such texts increasingly considered to represent textual constructions or reconstructions, as opposed to true records of the past. Of particular interest to contemporary scholars is the process of the construction of social or collective memory and, more specifically, the impact of traumatic historical events on its production. These questions are all pertinent to my analysis of the works studied here, as I discuss the ways in which the four writers in question position themselves in relation to the past—both personal and historical—and explore the role of memory in the construction of their narratives of the self. Moreover, their works are discussed in the context of the autobiographical tradition in Spain. The longstanding assumption that Spanish literary history lacks such a tradition and that few Spanish writers have chosen to engage in life-writing has been refuted by critics over recent years, as is discussed in chapter 1.[10]

While this book takes these four women as a group, drawing parallels between their life stories and their interactions with different aspects of their social environment, each writer is nevertheless studied separately, to avoid obscuring the individuality of each specific writer and her works. My opening chapter presents a framework for the study, outlining details of the relevant sociohistorical and political context and the processes of modernization that took place in Spain in the early twentieth century. In particular, the social situation of women during this period is discussed, with regard to the discourses of gender that prevailed at the time and the development of a women's movement in Spain. The literary history of the period in question is likewise examined, with a focus on the relationship of women writers to the dominant literary trends and movements of the day. Finally, discourses pertinent to life-writing and the workings of memory in narrative are explored, and these theories are again considered with regard to questions of gender.

Carmen Baroja's autobiographical narrative, *Recuerdos de una mujer de la generación del 98,* constitutes the focus of the second chapter, which discusses this author's depiction of her efforts to define for herself an identity in the public cultural arena in the face of overwhelming obstacles. Baroja's work reveals much about the reality of life for women of the upper and middle classes from the turn of the century through to the 1930s, particularly with regard to their exclusion from cultural endeavors.

Chapter 3 examines María Martínez Sierra's representation of the different facets of her past in her two autobiographical texts, *Una mujer por caminos de España* and *Gregorio y yo.* The author's portrayal of her complex positioning as a political figure and feminist activist, and as a writer who chose anonymity in the cultural arena, is explored in this section of my study. Martínez Sierra's depiction of her relationship to the gendered literary scene of early twentieth-century Madrid is also central to my analysis of her life-writing.

The fourth chapter of this study examines María Teresa León's *Memoria de la melancolía,* a work that opens up for discussion important questions about the workings of memory in the autobiographical process. Acknowledging the limits of remembering while simultaneously emphasizing the need to recall and articulate the past, León reflects on her own personal experiences and, in a broader sense, on those of her generation, celebrating the cultural wealth of Republican Spain and communicating the trauma of exile. León's representation of the relationship that she and her female contemporaries had with the gendered literary and cultural arena is also examined in this chapter.

The focus of the final chapter of this study is Concha Méndez's *Memorias habladas, memorias armadas,* a text in which the author recounts a life story marked by exclusion, in terms of gender marginalization, her exclusion from the literary center, and geopolitical exile. My discussion of Méndez's work centers on her representation of the position of women on the writing scene in 1920s and 1930s Madrid, as this author seeks quite explicitly to write herself into a literary history from which she has been excluded.

As will be seen in the ensuing analysis of the life-writing produced by Baroja, Martínez Sierra, León, and Méndez, the different experiences of these women—or at least, their textual representations of those experiences—point to the difficult relationship that women writers had with the gendered norms of the literary scene in early twentieth-century Spain. In works that might be described as narratives of the self, given that they diverge in certain respects from traditional conceptions of the autobiographical, these four writers reveal the complex interactions between women and modernity during a period of widespread social, cultural, and political change. In addition, their texts open up for discussion issues surrounding the role of memory in accessing and recounting the past and in the construction of narrative accounts of life stories.

1

The Woman Writer in Early Twentieth-Century Spain: Literary, Cultural, and Gender Politics

THE PROCESS OF MODERNIZATION THAT OCCURRED IN SPANISH SOCIETY in the first decades of the twentieth century resulted in significant changes in all aspects of life, from economic and social structures to the emergence of new cultural modes and values. Critical discourse about culture also reflected anxiety about changes in the role of women in society. While these decades brought new opportunities for women and a degree of social and intellectual freedom, female writers and intellectuals in early twentieth-century Spain neverthe-less encountered many obstacles in their efforts to transcend gender barriers and to participate in the literary and cultural scene of the day.

The first decades of the twentieth century are widely considered to have been one of the most fruitful and dynamic periods in Spanish literary history. The leading figures of the celebrated group known as the "Generation of 1898" were still active on the literary scene, at the same time as the younger writers who were to become known as the "Generation of 1927" emerged, a group considered to have produced some of the most exceptional poetry of the twentieth century. Within this group are such well-known figures as Federico García Lorca, Rafael Alberti, Luis Cernuda, and Vicente Aleixandre, among others. The efforts of these writers, and of their counterparts in other areas of the creative arts, are considered to have constituted a cultural renaissance of a kind unknown in Spain since the Golden Age of the sixteenth and seventeenth centuries; hence the designa-tion of this period as the *Edad de Plata,* or Silver Age, of Spanish liter-ature and culture.

Spanish literary history of the period from the turn of the century to the 1930s has come to be dominated by the male writers who have been considered to constitute these principal literary movements. In fact, the various "generations," as they have traditionally been termed, continue to be largely perceived to have been exclusively male domains, with no women figuring among the writers generally accepted to constitute these groups. For example, while there is a lack of critical consensus regarding "membership" of the poetic "Generation of 1927," with critics presenting differing views on the writers to be included and on the criteria for inclusion, there is general consensus that these poets were all male. Numerous canonical studies omit references to women writers of the period, while others make only brief mention of one or two female poets.[1] The absence of women from anthologies and literary histories is significant: while such reference works serve as indicators of those writers and works included in the canon, they are also implicated in the very process of canon formation.

The exclusion of women writers of this period from such texts is noted by critic José-Carlos Mainer, who observes that female literary figures "are conspicuous by their absence" (1989, 13) in literary studies, an absence which Mainer himself replicates in his text *La Edad de Plata* [The Silver Age] (1983), in which he does not include Méndez, Champourcin, or their contemporaries.[2] The few critical studies that do include women almost uniformly present them as peripheral figures, secondary to the group described by one critic as the "shining stars of contemporary Spanish poetry" (Infante 1986, 12). Despite the fact that Gerardo Diego did include two female poets of the period, Josefina de la Torre and Ernestina de Champourcin, in the 1934 edition of his well-known anthology, their incorporation into the canon proved to be temporary.

Furthermore, some recent studies which do specifically examine women's literary production in Spain tend to replicate traditional perceptions regarding female poets in the early twentieth century. Referring to the woman poet as "almost non-existent" in this period, Cristina Ruiz Guerrero goes on to make the following observation: "Our women poets cannot be reduced to these generational schemata, either because they are significantly absent in the moments when specific literary groups form, or because their production maintains a personal and independent line, on the margins of the modes that triumph, or because their development as writers is discontinuous, resisting classification" (1997, 186). Although they have not been deemed worthy of canonical inclusion and have indeed been considered to fall outside the generational groupings, it is clear that women writers were active on the literary scene during these periods of flourishing literary production. Moreover, some female poets of this period did deploy poetic techniques and express thematic concerns in their works that were similar to those found in works of their well-known male contemporaries and were, in fact, criticized for such "imitation," as Bellver has shown (1997b, 2001).

While much of the critical work with regard to this era focuses on poetry, due to the predominance of male poets of the time, it is important to note that women who wrote in other genres during this period have suffered similar neglect to that of female poets. While the silence surrounding these women has been questioned by a small number of critics in recent years—and I signal again here the importance of studies such as those by Bellver, Kirkpatrick, and Mangini—these writers nevertheless remain very much on the margins of literary history.

The canons on which Spanish literary history is based are premised on the concept of the above-mentioned literary "generation." The concept of categorizing literary periods according to generational schemata originates from the work of German critic Julius Petersen (1930) and was advanced in Spain in works published by Pedro Salinas (1941) and Pedro Laín Entralgo (1945), among others.[3] Despite much criticism of the generational model over recent decades, it continues to constitute the principal tool in the organization and valuation of Spanish literature, particularly that of the pre–Civil War period.[4]

Contemporary critics have challenged this continued use of what Michael Ugarte terms the "generational fallacy" (1994), a narrow and exclusionary literary historical model that, argues Christopher Soufas, "devalues national talents not identified within a privileged elite" (1998, 469).[5] The literary generation essentially consists of a small number of writers from a specific period who are deemed to best represent literary production of the era in question. As is the case with the formation of any canon, the process of selection and exclusion is subjective and arbitrary, reflecting ideological bias and resulting in the subsequent devaluation of those authors and works not included in such a category.[6] While some critics such as Vicente Gaos (1965) and Ángel González (1976) have proposed the use of the term *grupo poético* [poetic group] in place of *generación* [generation], such an alternative designation serves only to relabel the same concept, without challenging the notion on which it is premised.

If, then, we accept the arguments put forward by critics such as Ugarte and Soufas, who consider that continuing to refer to groups of writers and poets by terms such as *generación* and *grupo poético* maintains the exclusionary politics of this model, it appears redundant to argue for the inclusion of individual women writers in such groups. Such an approach would serve only to modify slightly the existing canon, without calling into question its validity. It is precisely such an expansion of the canonical "Generation of 1927" to include female poets that is advocated by Cole in his study (2000, 176). This approach constitutes an example of what Gerda Lerner has termed "contribution history": a strategy which serves to add details of women's lives to the male-dominated historical enterprise without challenging the existing framework (1976, 358). I argue that a more fundamental revision of the canon is necessary in order to broaden the scope of literary study and challenge the gendered politics of the generational model which dominates Spanish literary criticism. This involves not only revising the canon, centering figures who have been absent from or only marginally present in literary history, which is one of the implicit purposes of this study, but also evaluating the ways in which the field must be reconfigured as a result.

One of the major shortcomings of the generational model that has been identified by critics is the way in which it has isolated Spanish literary history from broader European cultural contexts. The artistic and literary scene throughout Europe in the first decades of the twentieth century was dominated by Modernism and by avant-garde cultural movements and, as Janet Pérez affirms, Spain was not immune to these trends: "Spain's 'new' intellectuals and literati were completely immersed in modernity as Europe conceived it" (1988–89, 40). Without eliding the complexity of the movement, in broad terms Modernism constitutes the artistic and literary response to modernity that developed during the period from 1890 to 1930, with literary Modernism characterized by the use of new artistic forms and an emphasis on individual consciousness.[7] There is, however, continued debate among scholars about the nature and extent of Modernism, and different understandings of this term have emerged in different contexts. It is not within the scope of this study to seek to define Modernism nor to enumerate the characteristics of literary production defined in this way. Such questions are addressed in numerous studies, with critics generally concurring that the term "Modernism" is too complex and diverse to encompass in a single definition. As Peter Brooker has affirmed, "[t]here is plainly

more than one modernism, and not all modernisms are equal"
(1992, 1).[8]

Spanish Modernism barely figures in analyses of European Modernism, with Peninsular literary production perceived as peripheral to the European movement. Important studies such as those by Malcolm Bradbury and James MacFarlane (1991) and Astradur Eysteinsson (1990) exclude Hispanic production, resulting in what Geist and Monleón describe as "an extremely distorted canon" (1999, xix). Critics such as Germán Gullón (1992) and John Butt (1980) have likewise criticized this omission, arguing for a broadening of understandings of Modernism to allow consideration of Spanish literature of the period within the wider context of international Modernism. These scholars point to the existence of a rich corpus of Modernist literature within the Hispanic world, noting particularly the influence of the writings of José Ortega y Gasset on discussions about Modernism and arguing against the exclusion of writers from both Spain and Latin America from discussions of the movement (Geist and Monleón 1999, xix).

The links drawn by these critics between Peninsular and Latin American Modernism are significant and derive largely from the important influence of Nicaraguan poet Rubén Darío's symbolist language on Hispanic literary trends. While Darío initially looked to France for intellectual and artistic models and declared the independence of Latin American Modernism from Castilian literary tradition, he came to adapt his stance in this regard later in his career. Following Spain's defeat in the Spanish-American War of 1898 and due to the increasing awareness of the imperial designs of the United States in Latin America, Darío came to identify more openly with Spain and with pan-Hispanic spiritual and cultural values, perceiving Spain and Latin America to be united in opposition to the United States and alluding to the increased cultural vitality evident in Spain by 1904. Critical tradition is divided on the question of the relationship between Spanish and Latin American Modernism. While some critics argue that a clear unity and commonality existed between the two movements, others refute the notion that such an affinity existed, insisting that a clear division exists between them.[9] Although there are undeniably differences between the movements, their links to each other and to European Modernism cannot be overlooked. However, the specificity of the sociocultural and political contexts in which literary production is immersed must certainly be taken into consideration.

In addition, some critics contend that there is a direct association between the exclusion of Peninsular literature from conceptions of Modernism and the generational model that negated the presence of this movement in Spain, an association that, they maintain, indicates that said absence originated, at least in part, in Spain itself. Soufas has argued that this is, moreover, considered to be closely linked to the ideological purposes of the Franco regime: "The poets of the 'Generation of 1927' were viewed as anything but Modernists because to have done so would have acknowledged Europe at a moment when Spain was actively shunning the Continent and exalting its own unity of national purpose" (1991–92, 267). Thus both traditional Spanish literary history and the Francoist state were premised on ideals of the separation of Spain from the rest of Europe and on a homogeneous vision of national unity. However, this refers to a retrospective negation of Modernism, developed to support the political objectives of the Franco regime. In fact, the "Generation of 1898" can be said to represent an early Modernism, as will be further discussed, while the "Generation of 1927" corresponds to a form of late Modernism.[10]

The fact that Modernism was a movement that developed outside of Spain and was thus viewed as representative of "foreign" influences resulted in its being deemed inferior to what was considered to be the truly "Spanish" style of the "Generation of 1898." As a result, Spanish literature of this period came to be viewed in terms of two opposing tendencies: the "Generation of 1898" and the new *modernismo*. The separation between these two groups has been rejected by many critics as inaccurate and arbitrary. Butt, for example, maintains that "the idea of two separate *modernista* [modernist] and *noventa y ocho* [1898] movements is an invention of later criticism which does not reflect the real complexities of the literature of the period" (1980, 137). Butt thus makes reference to the fact that the division between these literary modes was introduced retrospectively, arguing that in the first decades of the twentieth century no such division was perceived to exist. Rather, the terms "Generation of 1898" and "modernist" were used interchangeably, and it was not until the 1930s, with the emergence of generational theory, that these became strictly differentiated.[11] An alternative position is, however, held by María Dolores Dobón (1996), who contends that the writers of the period in question were fully aware of their separation into two distinct and opposing movements, each of which was characterized by different attitudes, concerns, and influences.

The differentiation of the two groups and the concomitant subordination of Modernism was developed in writings by Pedro Salinas in the 1930s and 1940s, and his theories were adopted and developed in the post–Civil War period by Pedro Laín Entralgo and Guillermo Díaz-Plaja.[12] Díaz-Plaja, for example, refers to these two groups as "two totally differentiated schools" (1951, 69–70), and sets out to differentiate systematically the two in his study, based on Petersen's criteria. More recent criticism rejects such a binary interpretation, which Richard Cardwell refers to as an "altogether false picture [that] has bedeviled any proper assessment of the real identity and role of Spanish *modernismo*" (2004, 502), going on to affirm that many of the works produced by the "Generation of 1898" "are in no little way shaped by the aesthetics of *modernismo*" (2004, 503). Similarly, Nil Santiáñez refers to canonical writers of the so-called "Generation of 1898," such as Valle-Inclán, Pío Baroja, and Unamuno, as the "great masters of Spanish Modernism" (2004). Following these contemporary critics, my study does not adopt the traditional approach of differentiation and seeks to avoid the use of such rigid labels and distinctions in its examination of the life-writing of the women studied.

The model of differentiation between the "Generation of 1898" and *modernismo* also invokes distinctions between the two groups based on gender difference, with the latter literary mode considered to be gendered feminine, in direct contrast to the energy and virility associated with the "Generation of 1898." As Guillermo Díaz-Plaja affirms, "we observe a series of elements allied to the masculine symbol in the Generation of 1898 and to the feminine symbol in *modernismo*" (1951, 211).[13] This formulation thus replicates the binary opposition male/female, with both *modernismo* and women clearly subordinated to their "masculine" counterparts. Moreover, Kirkpatrick draws a connection between the gendering of these literary movements and the purported division between them: "The association of *modernismo* with the feminine functioned effectively in the eventual splitting of Spain's literary modernism into the opposing tendencies of modernism—seen as a superficial and purely aesthetic movement—and the Generation of 1898, defined by 'its Spanishness, its virility, its ethics and the density of its thought'" (1999, 118–19). Such a tendency to assign to Modernism a feminine identity is ironic given the systematic exclusion of women from the Modernist canon, a contradiction that points to the shifting complexities of this literary and cultural movement in relation to gender politics.

The exclusionary ethics of the cultural models predominant in early twentieth-century Spain are often overlooked, due to the fact that movements such as Modernism and the avant-garde are considered to be characterized by a rejection of the existing order and by the promotion of disruptive, revolutionary cultural practices.[14] While the experimentation and creative freedom associated with these movements clearly provided a nurturing environment and a source of inspiration for some women, they were by no means free of patriarchal strictures. That the ideological assumptions underlying these cultural practices privilege a male subject position has been argued in studies by feminist critics such as Shari Benstock (1986, 1989) and Susan Rubin Suleiman (1990). Relating such notions to the Spanish context, Hispanist Maryellen Bieder has made the following affirmation: "It should not be forgotten that Modernism is a singularly male movement that in Spain as elsewhere excludes women and pushes women's writing outside the boundary of canonical literature" (1992, 314). It is the struggle for women to assert themselves within such an ambivalent cultural environment that the writers who form the basis of this study document in their life-writing.

In addition to the positioning of these women in relation to the dominant literary models of their day, consideration must be given to the sociohistorical and political environment of early twentieth-century Spain. While this study does not seek to provide a full historical account of the period in question, some background information on the social situation of women in Spain in the first decades of the twentieth century is essential to an understanding of the cultural situation of the female intellectual in Spain during this period. Moreover, the social position of women must be considered in the wider context of the social, political, and economic landscapes of the period.

Spanish political history of the nineteenth century is marked by social conflict and political instability. Over the course of the century, the traditional society dominated by landowners, the Bourbon monarchy, and the Catholic Church came to face increased opposition from secular groups who argued for the introduction of more modern "European" ideals, such as democracy, liberalization, and economic reform. While such groups attempted to transform Spain from an absolutist monarchy to a liberal constitutional system, the liberal political class was weak and its efforts to introduce change were frustrated by the continued opposition of the conservative ruling classes, who sought to preserve their political and economic interests. As a result, relatively little sustained development of social and economic structures took place during this period in Spain, in comparison with what occurred in other European countries.

However, economic historians have, over recent years, rejected the tendency to constantly compare the situation in Spain with that of other countries, a comparative trend that dominated nineteenth-century discourses on the nation and prevailed well into the twentieth century. As David Ringrose affirms, "[t]he assumptions that surround nationhood, and the positivist concept of 'progress,' have often lead to the conscious (or unconscious) assumption that there is a logical, normative, and even inevitable path that nations are destined to follow, if only because one or more have already done so" (1996, 24). Seeking to redress the widespread perception that the Spanish economy experienced only decline throughout the nineteenth century, Ringrose argues that, in fact, the economy underwent significant growth during this period, albeit at a slower rate than in other countries (1996, 56–80). Ringrose's thesis is echoed by Adrian Shubert, who emphasizes that Spain was simply a "laggard," rather than a failure (1990, 11). At the beginning of the twentieth century, then, Spain had experienced some economic growth, but continued to lack industrialization and modernization when compared to its European neighbors. In addition, the country was characterized by a highly centralized political system and by traditional, conservative social structures.[15]

The Catholic Church was a pervasive political institution during the period in question, and played a significant role in the shaping of cultural values in Spanish society. Although it is true that the Catholic Church also exerted much influence over society in some of Spain's European neighbors, most notably Italy and France, moves were made in those countries to secularize public life in the late nineteenth and early twentieth centuries. In Spain, however, the Church retained its authority in the social and political arenas well into the twentieth century, with the brief exception of the years of the Second Republic.

The ideology about women that dominated Spanish society in the late nineteenth and early twentieth centuries was, as a result, deeply influenced by Roman Catholic doctrine. It was an ideology based on a discourse that promoted the ideal of woman as a *perfecta casada* [perfect married lady]—a model initially advocated by Fray Luis de León in the sixteenth century—and as an *ángel del hogar* [angel of the home]. Central to these constructions was the notion that women are predisposed to a life of domesticity and maternal devotion, with marriage and motherhood constituting the two key components of women's cultural identity. The effective management of the house was perceived to be the foremost task of the *perfecta casada,* a role that in the nineteenth century was attributed a degree of social status and was considered to be a duty of vital social importance. However, the status associated with this role declined in the late nineteenth and early twentieth centuries. The definition of women as naturally belonging within the home nevertheless continued under the ideology of the *ángel del hogar,* summarized by Bridget Aldaraca in the following terms: "The ideal woman is ultimately defined . . . by the space which she occupies. The frontier of her existence as a virtuous woman begins and ends at her doorstep" (1991, 27). Moreover, such a formulation makes explicit the belief that a woman who transgresses the socially imposed boundary between the domestic enclave and the public arena is dishonorable.

Such an emphasis on the domestic responsibilities of women meant that paid work fell outside women's cultural identity as formulated by this model, thus reinforcing the ideology of separate spheres that defined the public arena of labor, politics, and culture as a masculine domain, assigning women to the private realm of the domestic. Some women did, of course, participate in the paid labor market in the pre–World War I era, although paid work for women was only deemed to be socially acceptable in the case of single women or due to economic necessity. Those women who did work outside the home tended to work in unskilled, poorly paid jobs and generally earned lower wages than their male counterparts. Female workers were particularly concentrated in the agricultural sector and in places of work such as textile and tobacco factories.[16] The incorporation of women into the workforce was perceived to represent a threat to the institution of the family, as it blurred the boundary between the public and private spheres and challenged the prevailing cult of domesticity that restricted women to the home.

Unsurprisingly, under this ideology women were considered to be inferior to men in what was a clearly defined hierarchical gender order, based on premises of biological essentialism, evidenced by the following affirmations made by Gener Pompeyo in the newspaper *La Vanguardia* in the late nineteenth century: "From her intelligence to her stature, everything about her is inferior and contrary to men . . . In herself a woman is not like a man, a complete being;

she is simply the instrument of reproduction, destined to perpetuate the species; while man is charged with its progress, the generator of intelligence, at once creator and demiurge of the social world" (1889). Such a model makes explicit that attributes of reason, creativity, and intellectual capacity were exclusive characteristics of men, and the lack of such qualities in women reinforced the view that they were "naturally" unsuited to the spheres of work, culture, and politics, but ideally suited to a life of dedication to the home and family. The insistence on these traits as "natural" implied that any woman who did not conform to such a model was, in fact, defying the norms of nature itself; she was, by extension, "unnatural," an aberration.

This discourse premised on the assumption of women's intellectual inferiority came to be replaced by a theory based on a concept of differentiation, which during the first decades of the twentieth century emerged as the prevalent model for theories of gender. During this period, the construction of gender difference came to be increasingly formulated on supposedly scientific foundations, with medical discourse functioning as an influential authority on issues of gender by the 1920s. The most prestigious figure in the shaping of scientific arguments to define women's role in society was Dr. Gregorio Marañón, an eminent endocrinologist whose writings on gender identity became central to dominant gender discourse. Marañón's scientific theories were considered to represent a more modern ideology than the religious-based ideals that had dominated theories of gender until this time, for his model did not posit women as inferior to men. Rather, Marañón contended that the sexes were of equal and complementary status, thus differentiating his theories from the prevailing ideology of domesticity.[17]

However, despite the apparently modern and egalitarian tendency of Marañón's theories, these were based around the key notion of gender difference—that is, Marañón argued that biological difference inevitably assigned different and complementary roles to men and women. For women, this role was motherhood. Women's social mission was to reproduce, and all other activities were to be subordinated to this primary duty: "There is no doubt that a woman should be a mother above all, forgetting everything else if necessary; and be so through the irrevocable obligation of her sex, just as a man should apply his energy to the task of creation, through the same irrevocable law of his masculine sexuality" (1926, 73). Marañón's theories thus perpetuated the traditional ideology of separate spheres and under his model women's cultural identity was constructed solely through the maternal role. Once again, participation in the paid workforce fell outside such a formulation, except in specific cases, such as that of the single woman. Marañón invoked, moreover, religious conceptions of gender difference, citing the Bible in his writings: "Again we hear the voice of God, insistent and eternal: 'You, woman will give birth; you, man, will work'" (1926, 73). Thus such supposedly "modern" and scientific theories continued to draw on the teachings of the Church in the area of gender discourse.

Despite the prevalence of such ideologies, the first decades of the twentieth century did see some changes in the status of and attitudes toward women, due to a number of factors: the influence of foreign models, including an awareness of the advances made by women in other countries; some improvement, albeit minimal, in educational opportunities available to women; and the incorporation of higher numbers of women into the workforce due to economic pressures, a factor which was exacerbated by the effects of the First World War.

Although Spain officially adopted a neutral stance in the war, this conflict nevertheless had significant social and economic consequences in Spain.[18] The lower-middle and working classes were negatively affected by the increased prices of goods, resulting in further discontent and social tension. In contrast, the more wealthy sectors of society experienced very favorable economic conditions as a result of the war. In fact, the period between 1914 and 1920 is considered to have definitively created a capitalist society in Spain (Roldán and García Delgado 1973). That this was a period of particular prosperity for the bourgeoisie is corroborated by Méndez's account of these years in her memoirs, as she recounts how her father's business flourished during the years of the First World War (1990, 31). In addition, the war resulted in an increase in the number of women in the workplace, as the increased production necessary for the war effort created jobs and the price increases of the period obliged more women to undertake paid work. The increased presence and visibility of women in the workforce added further impetus to the emerging debates about the role of women in Spanish society.[19]

In terms of political developments, the 1920s brought a repressive military regime to Spain, under the command of Gen. Miguel Primo de Rivera, who staged a coup in September of 1923 with the support of the army, conservatives, and King Alfonso XIII. Primo de Rivera established a program of reforms designed to improve the economy, but lost his support base when the economy failed to improve by the late 1920s. He resigned in January 1930, leaving Spain in a state of economic crisis and increasing political tension. When Republican candidates achieved overwhelming victory in the municipal elections held in April 1931, the Second Republic was declared, and Spain witnessed a brief period of democratic modernization, until the outbreak of the Civil War in July 1936.

The political events of the late 1920s and early 1930s that led to the fall of the monarchy and the proclamation of the Republic in 1931, the 1934 revolution in Asturias, and the eventual outbreak of the Civil War in 1936 inevitably affected the literary and cultural climate in Spain, as political and social issues were brought to the forefront of individual and national consciousness. While critics have stressed the generally apolitical nature of writers and artists in Spain during the Modernist period, with Ugarte noting that they were "not so much oblivious to social problems as brazenly indifferent" (1996, 107),[20] the political and economic reality of these years forced many into some form of political action and led to an aesthetic shift away from the more idealistic "art for art's sake" poetics of the 1920s toward a more politically committed position in the early 1930s. A significant number of writers, artists, and intellectuals dedicated their talents to political ends, and the vast majority of Spanish vanguard artists supported the left (Tusell 1999, 193). The connections that developed between culture and politics during these years were such that the Republic has been termed "the intellectuals' Republic" and the Civil War has been referred to as "the poets' war."[21] This association was similarly made explicit by Manuel Azaña y Díaz, president of the Second Republic in late 1931 and from May 1936 to February 1939, who referred to "politics as an art, with the people as the palette" (quoted in Thomas 1989, 35). The impact of the political events of this period on the literary community in Madrid is articulated, to varying degrees, in the life-writing of the women included in this study, and their works reveal the gender-specific ways in which they experienced these changes.

With regard to gender discourse, the early 1900s, and in particular the 1920s, designated the *años felices* [happy years] in Spain, saw the emergence of the figure of the *mujer nueva* [new woman], based on a gender model that was dominant in North America and in a number of European countries by this time. This new "modern woman" was characterized by a boyish image: she sported short hair, adopted new modes of dress, and participated in physical activities that had previously been the preserve of men—sports and aviation, for example. She was, moreover, an urban woman who was educated, had professional aspirations, and was interested in culture and politics; as such, she challenged traditional norms of feminine behavior.[22] As we will see, Concha Méndez was in many ways representative of this "modern woman."

The early twentieth century in Spain thus witnessed some modifications of traditional views of gender and a degree of blurring of the categories of masculinity and femininity, as women began to participate in areas that had been exclusively male domains, and figures such as the "new woman" and the dandy challenged conventional norms of masculine and feminine behavior. These developments were particularly felt in urban areas and among middle and upper class sectors of society, and thus cannot be held to reflect the experience of women of the period more generally. These changing visions of gender are, however, certainly pertinent to this study, due to my focus on Madrid and on the life-writing of four women with access to financial resources and links to the cultural world.

The emergence of such new models and attitudes notwithstanding, the vast majority of Spanish women continued to experience discrimination and inequality in cultural, economic, and social terms. The existing inequalities between men and women were enforced by Spain's legal framework, which was based on the gender prescriptions set down by the Napoleonic Code from the early nineteenth century. Married women, in particular, lacked any measure of independence under this legal structure, which established obedience to her husband as a wife's primary obligation, formulated in the Civil Code as follows: "A husband should protect his wife, and she should obey her husband" (quoted in Scanlon 1986, 127). A married woman had to reside where her husband decided and needed his permission for a wide range of activities, including entering into a contract, working, and buying or selling property. In terms of political rights, women were similarly in a disadvantageous position: until the reforms implemented by the Second Republic, women in Spain could not vote, nor could they stand as political candidates at either municipal or national level.[23]

While similar situations in terms of social and political rights existed for women in other European countries until at least the mid-nineteenth century and progress in the area of women's rights was gradual and uneven, by the first decades of the twentieth century significant progress had been made to improve women's legal and social status in most countries. In Spain, however, there was practically no reform of the gender laws set down in the Civil Code until the advent of the Second Republic in 1931.

The changes made by the Republic in this area were wide-ranging, as a whole package of social, cultural, and legal reforms were implemented. These sought to vastly improve women's civil and employment rights—introducing such major advances as divorce in 1932 and abortion in 1936—while acknowledging women as citizens with political rights.[24] From 1931, women could be nominated as political candidates and, following the establishment of the new Constitution, they were also granted the right to vote. In the first elections of the Republic in 1931, three women were elected as representatives to the *Cortes* [Parliament], a number which increased to five in the elections of 1933 and 1936. Despite such advances, overall the participation of women in the formal political arena was very limited.[25] The reforms implemented by the Republic were, moreover, short-lived, with the Franco regime reinstating much of the old Civil Code at the end of the Civil War in 1939. As a result, basic civil and political equality for women was not achieved in Spain until the late 1970s.

A feminist movement did develop in Spain in the early twentieth century, with a number of women's organizations emerging, supported mainly by women from the middle classes. However, the development of the feminist movement in Spain took place later than in other European countries, due to the slower growth of an urban middle class, the influence of the Catholic Church, and the generally traditionalist nature of Spanish society. It was also one of the weaker of the European feminist movements and was quite conservative in nature, as were those that developed in other Catholic countries in Europe. The focus of the women's organizations that were formed in Spain was to pursue increased civil and social rights for women, with a particular emphasis on issues associated with education. Political rights were not at the forefront of their concerns during this period.[26] As a movement based largely on what Mary Nash describes as "the social projection of motherhood and gender roles" (1994, 167), the influence of the feminist movement in Spanish society of the period proved to be minor and ineffectual.

Among the women's organizations formed in Spain in the early twentieth century, one of the most important was the Asociación Nacional de Mujeres Españolas [ANME; National Association of Spanish Women], established in 1918. While the ANME was quite conservative in political terms, as were most such groups at the time, the organization was in favor of women being granted the vote, and its policies did seek to improve the economic and social status of women, promoting improved educational and professional opportunities and advocating legal reform to end the discrimination against married women. Other organizations at the time that also advocated female political franchise included the Liga Internacional de Mujeres Ibéricas e Hispanoamericanas [International League of Iberian and Spanish American Women] and the Cruzada de Mujeres Españolas [Spanish Women's Crusade], both of which were led by well-known writer and feminist Carmen de Burgos.

In addition, women's organizations associated with different political groups developed, and the issue of women's rights emerged as a question of debate within the different political movements, particularly those on the left. While such groups theoretically supported the advancement of women, in practice they paid little attention to issues relating specifically to women's rights. In the case of the communists, such a stance was in line with the ideology of the movement, for it was believed that the class struggle was the primary goal and that the defeat of capitalism would result in the emancipation of women. This was the position argued by Communist leader Dolores Ibárruri, known as *La Pasionaria,* who was arguably the most prominent Spanish female political figure of the period.[27] Even within left-wing organizations, then, much discourse on gender replicated traditional ideology.

Women's participation in the political sphere was further hindered by the low level of education for women in this era and the corresponding high levels of illiteracy among the female population. While illiteracy rates were relatively high overall in Spain at this time, women fared worse than men: in 1900, the illiteracy rate for women was 71 percent, compared to 56 percent for men (Capel Martínez 1986, 363). These figures did improve over the first decades of the twentieth century, dropping to 47.5 percent for women and 37 percent for men by 1930, and there was increased acknowledgment of the need for improvement in the education of the female population.[28] Despite this, the education system up until the time of the Second Republic was strictly gendered, with classes for female students reflecting the prevailing ideology about women, serving to prepare them for a life of religious piety and dedication to their responsibilities as wives and mothers. Policies on education drew not only on the discourse of domesticity, but also on that of women's inferiority; as one scholar writing in the *Revista de España* in 1885 affirmed, women were believed to be "less apt for certain studies than men," in particular for work in fields such as philosophy and mathematics, due to the fact that these require "a great application of reason" (García Navarro 1885, 541).

In the sphere of higher education, the presence of women was minimal, with only a handful of women attending university before the turn of the century. These few female students were only admitted with special permission and under strict restrictions that kept them separated from their male classmates. In addition, many courses of study remained closed to women until 1910, when some legal reforms were implemented.[29] Although the situation in this area also improved somewhat over the following two decades, the number of female university students remained low, and few women went on to establish careers after completing their studies.

Despite this disheartening situation regarding educational opportunities for women, there are isolated examples of centers of cultural and intellectual activity that were established specifically to encourage female participation in the cultural sphere. As might be expected, such centers tended to be the preserve of a minority of comparatively well-educated women who often had ties to the cultural world—members of what Bellver has termed "the female cultural elite" (2001, 35). These were also, of course, developments that took place in an urban context, concentrated in Madrid and Barcelona.[30]

One such center was the Residencia de Señoritas [Young Women's Residence], the women's counterpart of the famed male-dominated Residencia de Estudiantes [Students' Residence]. Established in Madrid in 1915 under the direction of María de Maeztu, the Residencia de Señoritas sought to encourage women's participation in advanced education, by providing accommodation for female students in Madrid. Its significance, however, went well beyond that of a simple student hall of residence. The Residencia de Señoritas had a very specific cultural and educational purpose, with lectures, poetry readings, and musical and theatrical recitals held regularly for the benefit of its female residents, leading Carmen de Zulueta and Alicia Moreno to affirm that the Residencia "represented the greatest advance until the present day in the education of Spanish women" (1993, 209).[31]

Close ties were established between the Residencia de Señoritas and the Residencia de Estudiantes, allowing female students to benefit from the cultural vitality of the latter institution. It was, however, the masculine domain of the Residencia de Estudiantes that was to play a key role in the fomenting of arts and literature during this period. The importance of the Residencia de Estudiantes as a center of cultural and intellectual activity in Spain between 1910 and 1936 cannot be overlooked. Described by John Crispin as "one of the most prestigious cultural centers in Europe" (1981, 11), this institution was highly significant in the cultural life of Madrid, serving as a center for lectures by artists and scholars, poetry readings, and other recitals and artistic events. The Residencia de Estudiantes was, however, primarily a space of male intellectual activity from which women tended to be excluded, a marginalization made explicit by Méndez in her memoirs.

The Lyceum Club was another very important center for women that was prominent in Madrid in the decade preceding the outbreak of the Civil War. Established in 1926 following the model of Lyceum Clubs already founded in cities such as New York, London, and Paris, the Club's stated aim was to "defend the moral and material interests of women" in the broadest of terms (*Lyceum Club* 1929, 3). This involved the organization of activities ranging from community work to aid women of lesser means, to lecture presentations on cultural and literary topics. The Lyceum Club of Madrid proved to be very popular, with its membership increasing from 150 to 450 between 1926 and 1929, prompting the establishment of a branch in Barcelona in 1931 (Fagoaga 1985, 183–84). Among the Lyceum Club's members were women who were active on the political scene, ranging from socialists to members of the more conservative Asociación Nacional de Mujeres Españolas, while many other women who participated in the activities of the Lyceum Club were not directly involved in any political movement.

The importance of the Lyceum Club in providing a space specifically for women to gather and exchange ideas is emphasized in the writings of a number of women of the period, including Baroja and Méndez. Described as "the high point of the new feminine atmosphere of the era" by Marcia Castillo Martín (2001, 98), the Lyceum provided a unique opportunity for the development of a cultural space organized by and for women, at a time when the majority of centers of intellectual activity were closed to them. Perhaps unsurprisingly, the Lyceum Club was the target of much criticism from conservative sectors of society, including the Church. Described as a "real calamity for the home and natural enemy of the family" (quoted in Rodrigo 2002, 46), the Club was perceived to represent a threat to decent bourgeois society, challenging as it did the gendered boundaries of cultural activity. The establishment of the Lyceum Club also divided the emergent women's movement in the capital; as Pilar Nieva de la Paz affirms, "the conservative sector of the feminine movement never wanted to have anything to do with the center" (1993, 68). The reaction of members of Madrid's male literary elite to the Club was also varied; while writers such as Lorca, Unamuno, and Alberti presented lectures at the Lyceum, others were less supportive, most notably Benavente, whose description of the Lyceum Club members as *"tontas y locas"* [fools and madwomen] is now infamous.[32]

Organizations such as the Lyceum Club, together with the other centers of cultural activity of the period such as the Residencia de Estudiantes and the more informal tradition of the *tertulia* [social gathering], were important sites of intellectual practice and of collective participation in early twentieth-century Madrid. While women were excluded from some of these social spaces, the writers included in this study nevertheless signal in their life-writing the significance of these centers as potentially productive sites for the female intellectual, as will be discussed in the chapters that follow. These centers may be considered to constitute examples of what Pierre Nora designates *lieux de mémoire* or mnemonic sites, places that, Nora argues, for writers and intellectuals of a given period "form the fabric of their provisional identities and stake out the boundaries of their generational memories" (1996, 526).

It is this "generational" or social element of memory that Nora foregrounds in his writings, and this is a question that has received much attention from contemporary critics. The pioneering work in this area was Maurice Halbwachs's *On Collective Memory*, first published in French in 1950 and appearing in English in 1992. Halbwachs's theorization of memory as a collective, social phenomenon, as opposed to a purely individual one, has become tremendously popular in recent decades and has had far-reaching implications. Insisting that any memory is inevitably a social construct, Halbwachs argues that people construct memory not as individuals but as members of a society, and that they recall those memories in society.

All of the works examined in this book, as narrative accounts of life stories, are based upon and, in fact, made possible by memory. Assumptions about the way memory functions and the access it can give to the past are central to the autobiographical and cultural discourses discussed in this study. Theory on this question has been dominated by two contrasting or opposing models of memory. The first of these, developed by Freud in his writings on hysteria and traumatic memory, likens memory to archaeological excavation, positing it as a process of digging through the deposits of time to unearth an unchanging collection of facts. This notion that the past can be unproblematically recovered intact by the remembering subject, untouched by the passing of time and subsequent lived experience, is negated by the second model, which presents the process of memory as one of continuous revision, reshaping, and reinvention.[33]

It is this second model that has come to dominate criticism. It is now widely accepted that while autobiography is a form of writing that lays claim to factuality, it is by nature a process of creation that involves the selection and shaping of a life story. The observation made by Susannah Egan that the autobiographer, "unable to lift anything out of life and into art without transforming it . . . creates . . . a fictive self to narrate the events of his life and a fictive story to contain those events" (1984, 66), encapsulates the view expressed in much critical writing. The self and past of the autobiographical text are not remembered, but constructed, with the partial evidence available through memory. As such, life-writing is not and cannot be referential of a life or of past experiences; as James Olney notes, reference in life-writing "is never to events of the past but to memories of those events" (1998, 7). It is thus memory itself, as opposed to the writing self, which is proposed by Olney as the very subject of life-writing.

However, while autobiography is generally accepted to be fictive, and the requirement for what Elizabeth Bruss refers to as the "truth-value" of the "autobiographical act" (1976) has been discarded by most theorists, there nevertheless remains an expectation of some level of truthfulness in autobiographical writing. As Jonathan Loesberg affirms, redesignating autobiographical texts works of fiction "affront[s] our intuitive notion that autobiographies do not feel to the reader precisely like fiction" (1981, 174). A perceived intention on the part of the writer, then, to present an honest account of his or her past based on memory remains an important feature of life-writing.[34]

This question of factuality remains a primary concern for many authors of life-writing, and this is closely associated with the assumption that it is possible to represent the self and its experiences in narrative. Despite critics' affirmations that memories are "dynamic and constructed," as opposed to "static and mimetic," Paul John Eakin contends that "[t]he overwhelming majority of autobiographers continue to place their trust in the concept of an invariant memory that preserves the past intact" (1999, 107). Many autobiographical narratives thus negate or ignore memory as a process, presenting the past as wholly accessible to the remembering subject. As such, the narrating "I" and the "I" who is the subject of the narrative are presented as identical, in accordance with the notion of the "autobiographical pact" advanced by Philippe Lejeune (1989). The impossibility of such continuity of identity and the concomitant inevitable split between the two voices—that is, between the past and present selves—has been signaled by narrative theorists, and this division is a key question in my analysis of the life-writing examined in this book.

A related area of significance for this study is discourse surrounding the recalling and inscribing of traumatic events in one's past. Much contemporary work in this field focuses on the context of Holocaust memory and trauma, and the ways in which memories of this event are reconstructed in narrative.[35] Within the context of twentieth-century Spanish history, the Spanish Civil War must be considered a watershed event, an episode whose repercussions have been omnipresent in the cultural memory of Spain. While the focus of this book is on the period preceding the war, all of the autobiographical works studied were written in the post–Civil War era. Moreover, the lead-up to and consequences of the war inevitably shape, albeit in different ways and to varying degrees, the life stories and thus the narratives produced by Baroja, Martínez Sierra, León, and Méndez. Critical work in this area is thus pertinent to this study, and is drawn upon particularly in chapter 4 with regard to León's *Memoria de la melancolía*.

The discourses associated with life-writing outlined above, and discussed further in the chapters that follow, are inevitably informed by the gender politics that influence the construction of any cultural field. For women, life-writing has provided a vehicle for the voicing and preservation of stories and memories that have long been excluded from hegemonic discourses of cultural and collective memory. While feminist scholars have argued for many years that gender as a cultural construction cannot be evaded by any critical perspective, much theoretical work on life-writing and memory continues to ignore questions of gender. That women's autobiographical production has been neglected and denigrated by traditional critics has been well-documented in studies by feminist scholars published over recent years, and feminist approaches to autobiography have resulted in a reevaluation of traditional assumptions surrounding this form of writing.[36] Such works reveal that women's life-writing has been excluded from traditional autobiographical criticism and that women's memories have been, and continue to be, largely absent in the process of the construction of cultural memory.

Much contemporary discourse around autobiography continues to center on the disputed parameters of this form of writing, with traditional definitions of the genre excluding forms of life-writing such as diaries and letters that are often adopted by women and other groups deemed to fall outside mainstream literary culture. The preoccupation with the "conditions and limits" of autobiography is longstanding, as critics have sought to establish it as "a solidly established literary genre" (Gusdorf 1980, 28), configured as unquestionably white, male, and Western. The question of what constitutes autobiography "proper" pervades discussions about this form of writing, with the traditional canon differentiating autobiography from memoirs and diaries, in accordance with the formal definition of autobiography proposed by Lejeune: "Retrospective prose narrative written by a real person concerning his own existence, where the focus is his individual life, in particular the story of his personality" (1989, 4). Autobiography is thus formulated as a continuous prose account of the totality of the life of a "significant" individual who is, Jelinek contends, "a mirror of his era" (1980a, 7). The problematic nature of this exclusionary canon is articulated by Leigh Gilmore, who affirms that insistence on the generic boundaries of autobiography "must be seen as participating in the cultural production of a politics of identity, a politics that maintains identity hierarchies through its reproduction of class, sexuality, race, and gender as terms of 'difference' in a social field of power" (1994, 5).[37]

Within the Spanish context relevant to this study, questions of generic definition have likewise dominated much critical discussion of autobiography. While María Antonia Álvarez has, for example, signaled the similarities between different forms of life-writing, she nevertheless contends that it is possible to "define the frontiers that exist between them" (1989, 444). Similarly, Randolph Pope affirms that the texts selected for inclusion in his study of Spanish autobiographies produced between the fifteenth and eighteenth centuries were chosen based on "a strict criterion as to what constitutes an authentic autobiography" (1974, 294). Pope's work, together with those by Nicholas Spadaccini and Jenaro Talens (1988), Antonio Lara Pozuelo (1991), and Caballé (1995), among others, have served to discredit traditional assumptions that autobiography has long constituted a desert-like area of Spanish literature. Such an assumption is expressed by Rafael Alberti, a prominent figure on the Spanish literary scene in the period pertinent to this study, who affirms in his memoirs *La arboleda perdida* [The Lost Grove] that "in Spanish literature there are very few books of memoirs" (1987, 9). This widely held view is, however, refuted by critics, with Caballé, for example, confirming "the abundant corpus of memoirs which exists within Spanish literature in general" (1998, 111).

Furthermore, the increased critical attention dedicated in recent decades to autobiographical works produced in the post–Civil War era has revealed the existence of a significant corpus of previously neglected life-writing. Many of these texts were written from exile and a significant number are political in intent. Among these are testimonial accounts of Spanish women's experiences of war, politics, and exile, works that are designated "memory texts" by Mangini (1995). Interest in these works has opened up to scholars the field of life-writing by Spanish women, an area that was, until recently, largely unexplored.[38] Of particular relevance to this study is Christina Dupláa's work on history and memory and on testimonial writing in her studies of works by Montserrat Roig and Josefina Aldecoa, respectively (1996, 2000). In the former text, Dupláa, positing testimonial writing as a tool to "recover a past and re/construct it" (1996, 21), argues for a broader understanding of the form of writing known as the *testimonio*. Refuting assumptions that the *testimonio* is specific to the Latin American context, Dupláa seeks to emphasize "the universal value of its denunciation" and its relevance in diverse contexts in which "processes for the omission of voices have been developed for political reasons" (1996, 25). Questions related to the *testimonio* and collaborative life-writing projects are explored in chapter 5 in my discussion of Méndez's *Memorias habladas, memorias armadas*.

These questions relating to autobiographical discourses and the role of memory in life-writing are pertinent to the works of Baroja, Martínez Sierra, León, and Méndez that are examined in the following chapters. The accounts of the past produced by these four writers open up for discussion important questions regarding the workings of memory, including the ways in which it is reconstructed in narrative and implicated in notions of self-identity. Moreover, their works provide significant insights into the social and cultural reality of early twentieth-century Spain for the woman writer and intellectual, as they recount their efforts to transcend the gendered barriers of the cultural arena.

2

Carmen Baroja y Nessi (1883–1950), *Recuerdos de una mujer de la generación del 98:* Negotiating the Discourse of Domesticity

THE MEMOIRS OF CARMEN BAROJA Y NESSI ARE THE EARLIEST WRITTEN, YET most recently published, of the texts included in this study. Penned by Baroja in the early 1940s, the manuscript was only published in 1998, edited by Amparo Hurtado. The title of Baroja's work, *Recuerdos de una mujer de la generación del 98,* signals the literary circle with which this author, in some respects, aligned herself. Her text, however, documents the extent to which the restrictions placed on women in late nineteenth and early twentieth-century Spain served to exclude them from cultural and intellectual endeavors, as Baroja recounts her continual struggles with the identity prescribed for her by social convention. It is Baroja's textual inscription of her efforts to transcend the gendered boundaries of cultural activity, and the reflective self-analysis that her account entails, that will be examined in this chapter.

Baroja, born in Pamplona in 1883, was the youngest child in a family that already had three sons, one of whom was to die in his early twenties, with the other two becoming prominent artists and writers. During Baroja's childhood and adolescence, her family moved many times, before settling in Madrid in 1898. In these early years, Baroja received an education typical for girls of her social class, attending Catholic girls' schools and also having private tuition in French and music. Thanks to her father's love of the theater and music, the young Baroja regularly attended concerts and theatrical productions with her parents. While this period of Baroja's life gave the author her first taste of the cultural world, she does not discuss these years in any detail in her memoirs, which focus on her life in Madrid from 1898 on.

It was in the Spanish capital as a teenager that Baroja began to

46

participate in the cultural life of Madrid, attending art exhibitions and theatrical productions with her brothers. At this time, both her brothers were gaining prominence on the cultural scene, with Ricardo becoming recognized as a painter and Pío having his first literary works published. Through them, Baroja came into contact with numerous artists, writers, and intellectuals who were to become well-known figures in the cultural history of Spain. During the first decade of the twentieth century, Baroja also developed her own artistic inclinations in the area of metal and enamel work, gaining critical recognition for her works and winning a number of prizes. She spent six months in France on a study tour with Pío, and persuaded Ricardo to share his workshop with her and to help her develop her metal work skills.

However, despite these achievements, it is clear from Baroja's text that such activities were always considered by her family to be secondary to her domestic roles, as she describes the very traditional life her mother had planned for her and the different moral codes that operated for men and women in this sociohistorical context. In her work, Baroja is highly critical, not only of her mother and of her social environment, but also of her two brothers, whose egotism she highlights in her text. In fact, Baroja's presentation of her past in *Recuerdos* is, for the most part, overwhelmingly negative, as she summarizes her life in the following terms: "Las preocupaciones empezaron pronto y siguieron sin apartarse, por eso, al mirar atrás, veo un camino recto, seguido, largo, aburrido, larguísimo, monótono, siempre igual, con desgracias de vez en cuando y apenas una pequeña sonrisa" [The worries began early and continued without leaving me, so that, on looking back, I see a straight path, continuous, long, boring, extremely long, monotonous, always the same, with misfortunes from time to time and scarcely one little smile] (1998, 44).

The restrictions placed on Baroja as a young woman intensified following her marriage in 1913 to Rafael Caro Raggio, who, like the rest of her family, expected Baroja to conform to traditional models of womanhood. It is significant that Baroja dedicates very little space in her memoirs to the early years of her marriage—in fact, the period from 1913 to 1925 is covered in just half a page. While many important events in Baroja's life did take place during these years—the births of three of her children, two of whom died at the ages of four years and eighteen months respectively;[1] the establishment of her husband's publishing company, the Editorial Caro Raggio; his problems with depression; the economic difficulties faced by the family—the author signals that the memories of this part of her past are too painful to recall and recount.

Baroja's account of her past resumes in 1926, with a section of her memoirs that reveals the positive opportunities for women that emerged with the changing gender dynamics of the 1920s. It is in this period that Baroja once again came to participate in cultural life, albeit in a limited fashion due to the restrictions placed upon her by her husband. Baroja's involvement in both El Mirlo Blanco, the theatrical group that staged productions in the home of her brother Ricardo and his wife, Carmen Monné, and in the Lyceum Club, proved to be key for the development of her cultural identity and allowed her to be reincorporated into a social circle that went beyond the purely domestic.

In the 1930s and early 1940s, Baroja dedicated some of her time to writing, publishing a nonfictional work entitled *El encaje en España* [Lacemaking in Spain] (1933), and a work of fiction for children, *Martinito, el de la Casa Grande* [Little Martin From the Big House] (1942). She also wrote a number of articles for the magazine *Mujer,* which were generally published under her penname of Vera de Alzate.

Unlike her contemporaries who are included in this study, Baroja was not a fervent supporter of the Republic, expressing some misgivings about the end of the monarchy in Spain. In fact, her positioning with regard to the political events of the 1930s is somewhat ambiguous. The author does not appear to hold strong political views, and she is critical of both sides in her discussions of the Spanish Civil War. Baroja was certainly not active in the political sphere, and her text makes clear that political events were of no great interest to her, beyond the consequences that they had for her life and that of her family.

It is thus the effects of the Civil War on her daily life that Baroja represents in *Recuerdos.* She spent this period in the family's holiday home, known as Itxea, in Vera de Bidasoa in the Basque Country, together with her two sons and other family members, but separated from her husband. Baroja recounts the hardship of the war years, as well as the economic difficulties faced by the family following their return to the Spanish capital when the conflict was over. In contrast with the other three women studied here, Baroja did not go into exile, and as such her account offers the perspective of a woman who experienced the immediate post–Civil War period in Spain.

Baroja's account, which she finished writing in 1946, closes on a positive note. Now a widow, living with her brother Pío and her two sons, Baroja indicates that a new era of her life has started, despite the fact that she has lost much of what she had prior to the Civil War. This positive attitude to the future further emphasizes Baroja's negative portrayal of much of her past. Apart from writing her memoirs, Baroja also wrote poetry during the last years of her life, works that were published posthumously in an edition prepared by her son, Pío Caro Baroja, under the title *Tres Barojas* [Three Barojas] (1995). In addition, Baroja prepared two museum catalogues in the 1940s for the *Museo del Pueblo Español: Catálogo de la colección de amuletos* [Catalogue of the Amulet Collection] (1945) and *Catálogo de la colección de pendientes* [Catalogue of the Earrings Collection] (1948–52), thus continuing her interest in craftwork. These were Baroja's last publications; she died in Madrid in June 1950.

Recuerdos de una mujer de la generación del 98 is an autobiographical text that provides valuable insights into the constraints faced by women with intellectual interests in Spain from the turn of the century through to the 1930s. It is a work that, in a number of ways, does not conform to the canon of autobiographical writing, despite Bettina Pacheco's description of Baroja's text as a "true" autobiographical account. This critic maintains that "we are faced with an autobiography, properly speaking, every time that self-analysis is privileged over the narration of events or anecdotes outside the 'I'" (2001, 229), thus replicating traditional formulations of autobiography as distinct from memoirs or other forms of life-writing. This characterization of *Recuerdos*, however, overlooks some important elements of Baroja's work.

First, the fact that Baroja's account does not detail the early years of her life separates it from a conventional autobiography, which narrates the author's life from birth onward. Second, the process that led to the text's publication is atypical, with the role played by editor Amparo Hurtado of significance here. Baroja's manuscript had languished in her family's archives for several decades, and it was on Hurtado's initiative that the work was prepared for publication. It is clear from Hurtado's description of the editorial process in her prologue to the memoirs that the task of fashioning Baroja's manuscript into a readable narrative went well beyond simply making superficial corrections to spelling and clarifying references that might not be clear to the modern reader. Describing the original text as "un *puzzle* desmontado" [a dismantled puzzle] (1998b, 37;

italics in original), Hurtado notes that it was comprised of a bundle of papers of different sizes and colors, some typed and others handwritten, without any margins or page numbers (1998b, 13). Confirming that, as it stood, Baroja's text would not have been easy for a reader to follow, Hurtado describes her own task as constituting the "reconstruction" of the narrative in order to produce the text as it appeared in print (1998b, 14).

While Hurtado emphasizes that she did not make significant changes to Baroja's manuscript when transcribing the narrative, affirming that the work remains faithful to the original text (1998b, 37), her role nevertheless inevitably involved making certain editorial decisions that impacted on the final form of the text. For example, the memoirs have been ordered chronologically, following autobiographical convention, although we cannot be sure of the final decisions regarding the ordering of her narrative that Baroja may have made. While she does note her general intentions regarding the structuring of her account in her manuscript, indicating that she intended to follow a general chronological pattern, she does not divide her narrative into five distinguishable sections as she had planned. This discrepancy is acknowledged by Hurtado in a footnote in which the editor signals that Baroja did not, in fact, follow precisely her initial outline for her work (1998b, 49).

Further questions related to authorial intent are also raised by the process of publishing, as it is unclear whether Baroja would have sought to publish her work as it stood or if she perhaps considered these original pages to be a first draft of a future work. That Baroja's memoirs appear to be incomplete is similarly signaled by Castillo Martín, who affirms that *Recuerdos* "does not even constitute a completed work but, rather, is an unfinished project" (2001, 98). There are, for example, indications in Baroja's writing that she saw her work as unfinished. Referring to the period from 1913 to 1925, the years of her marriage that she does not recount in any detail in her memoirs, Baroja notes that "[m]e cuesta mucho recordar y más todavía anotarlo. Acaso con el tiempo lo consiga, pero por ahora es para mí muy molesto" [it is very hard for me to remember and even harder to write it down. Perhaps with time I shall achieve it, but for now it is very uncomfortable for me] (1998, 81). This leaves open the possibility that Baroja intended to return to this section at a later date, if she felt disposed to do so. The task of remembering and reconstructing her past is thus posited as an ongoing process, suggesting that her work is an unfinished product and that memory writing represents a potential way of seeking to leave the past behind.

Closely associated with these issues of authorial intent is the question of the possible audience being addressed by Baroja in *Recuerdos*. Once again, it is important to bear in mind here that it is unclear whether Baroja intended her work to be published, and thus be received by a wider audience, or if she meant her reflections on her life to remain within the family. In this latter case, Baroja may have sought to deploy the genre of life-writing to give herself a voice in a family dominated by male intellectuals and to make her relatives aware of the extent to which her own identity as an artist had been neglected. However, since Baroja did not prepare her manuscript for publication, she may not, in fact, have had a specific audience for her work in mind. Rather, the autobiographical act may have been something of a cathartic process in itself, an act of self-expression that allowed Baroja to reflect on her past. As such, *Recuerdos* may be read as an exploration or construction of selfhood and identity, written not for others, but for the benefit of the writing subject herself. Conversely, if Baroja did indeed intend her work for publication, part of her motivation may have been a desire to address the intellectual community from which she as a woman was excluded, and to highlight her identification with the literary and cultural "generation" of her time.

The issue of Baroja's somewhat tenuous relationship with the cultural world and her association with the canonical "Generation of 1898" is central to her self-portrayal in *Recuerdos* and is key to the identity that she inscribes in her work. While Baroja is critical of her brothers in her memoirs, it is undeniable that her family connections were instrumental in allowing her the limited contact with the literary and cultural world that she did achieve, opportunities that arguably would not have been available to her without them. With Ricardo and Pío, as well as with her parents, Baroja regularly attended theatrical performances, concerts, the opera, and art exhibitions, and cultural matters were a frequent topic of conversation within the family.

In addition, Baroja came into contact with many prominent writers of the period, such as Valle-Inclán and Azorín, and it is her association with this select circle of intellectuals at the turn of the century that leads Baroja to express an identification with the male-dominated "Generation of 1898." The author affirms that "los gustos, las ideas y el carácter todo mío lleva el sello de lo que yo supongo que era esta época" [the tastes, ideas, and character so much my own bear the stamp of what I consider this era to have been], while simultaneously conceding that the title of her work may be considered to be something of a "pedantería" [pedantry] (1998, 46). However, Pacheco argues that, despite this disclaimer, Baroja did indeed consider herself to form part of the "Generation of 1898." This critic maintains that through her text, Baroja sought to write herself into the literary record from which she had been excluded: "In spite of the *humilitas retórica* with which she excuses herself for choosing to entitle her text 'Memoirs of a Woman of the Generation of '98,' by this she is simply trying to conceal her intention to claim her rightful place in the midst of intellectuals and men of letters, among whom only masculine names figure" (2001, 227).

It is important to bear in mind here that Baroja was only fifteen years old in 1898 and was not to become a published writer until the 1930s. She therefore did not publish in the years immediately following 1898, when many of the key texts produced by members of the "generation" appeared, nor did she participate fully in the cultural activities of the period.[2] Also significant, however, is the fact that the label "Generation of 1898," identifying the historical events of that specific year as having given impulse to the movement, was developed retrospectively, and thus the year itself is to some extent arbitrary.

In any case, it seems to me that rather than an insistence that she be considered a "member" of this canonical group, Baroja's work suggests a more general identification with the "generation" and an awareness of the influence of the intellectual atmosphere of the time on her formation. Her text signals that the connections she had with the intellectual world as a young woman were significant in her life, as she points to the importance of the fact that she came of age in that specific intellectual environment, evidenced by her affirmation that the "generation" "en mí coincide con el despertar de las aficiones a la lectura, a las cosas artísticas" [coincides in me with the awakening of a passion for reading, for artistic things] (1998, 47). Baroja's narrative thus suggests that she considers this environment to have been formative and, at least to some extent, defining of her identity.

In summary, then, while Baroja clearly felt an affinity with the writers of the "Generation of 1898" and seeks to document in her text her intellectual interests and talents that were so often neglected, she does not present herself as an integral member of this canonical group.[3] Rather, Baroja's account emphasizes her positioning on the periphery of this male-dominated cultural world and contrasts her situation to that of her brothers.

Despite the fact that Ricardo and Pío were, in many respects, Baroja's models, she is critical of them and expresses her bitterness at the different rules that applied to them as men. Free from domestic responsibilities, they were able to focus from a young age on the cultural and intellectual pursuits in which they were interested. It is particularly this freedom that enabled them to participate in the cultural world that Baroja resents, as she notes the stark contrast between the life that they enjoy and in which she also wishes to partake, and the limited activities in which she is able to engage. She notes that from a young age she felt divided between these two worlds, resulting in a split sense of identity that, Baroja maintains, remained with her throughout her life: "Mi espíritu cada vez se iba dividiendo más entre la vida cotidiana, que sin duda era estúpida y aburrida, y lo que yo pensaba; entre mis amigas y mis conocimientos de la clase media . . . y mis lecturas y lo que yo hubiera querido hacer" [All the time my spirit was becoming more divided between daily life, which without doubt was stupid and boring, and what I was thinking; between my girlfriends and my middle class acquaintances . . . and my readings and what I would have liked to do] (1998, 56).

Both Ricardo and Pío adopted their mother's very traditional ideas about the role of women in society, according to Baroja, and did little to help their sister realize her own aspirations. She makes numerous references to their selfishness and their general lack of concern for others, opinions which are encapsulated in the following affirmation: "El egoísmo de Pío siempre ha sido terrible . . . A Ricardo le pasa igual [con] el egoísmo y la roñosería" [Pío's selfishness has always been terrible . . . Ricardo is the same, with his selfishness and meanness] (1998, 54). Baroja's comments with regard to her brothers' conservative ideas on women and the family, together with her criticism of their treatment of her, contradict the portrayal of her family by some critics and biographers. In particular, scholars of the life and work of Pío Baroja have often emphasized his "sympathy as regards the feminine sex" (Pérez Ferrero 1972, 160) and the mutual adoration that Pío and his sister felt toward one another (Pérez Ferrero 1972, 310).

Furthermore, Baroja's narrative makes explicit that she certainly did not always agree with her brothers' views. She affirms, for example, that she considered Pío's ideas to be traditionally "Spanish" in certain respects, despite his rejection of such a label (1998, 68). With regard to Ricardo, Baroja comments on her disapproval of his participation in political activity (1998, 96). Her assertiveness in discussions with her more educated brothers, which clearly goes against the grain in their familial and social environment, is similarly noted by Julio Caro Baroja, who affirms that his mother "had a great influence over my uncles. She was the only person who discussed judgments and opinions with them with a certain intensity" (1992, 64).

Baroja thus formulated and expressed her own opinions with regard to friends and acquaintances, the literary merits of prominent writers of the day, and social developments, as well as on the subject of literary innovations: "She was the first one at home who decided to buy an anthology of modern poetry, an odious thing for my uncle Ricardo, and for which my uncle Pío felt absolute indifference" (Julio Caro Baroja 1992, 64). Such examples indicate that Baroja did achieve a measure of independence, albeit only in terms of her thoughts and ideas, and further signal the author's efforts to define her own identity, beyond the limited roles assigned to her.

Nevertheless, Baroja's access to the cultural world of turn-of-the-century Madrid was inevitably both temporary and limited. She was only able to participate in gatherings that were held in her home and to attend expositions and other public events when accompanying her brothers. Other sites of intellectual debate were closed to her, such as the *tertulias* in which her brothers and their contemporaries regularly participated. The importance of these gatherings is signaled by her brother Ricardo in his work *Gente del 98* [People of the Generation of 1898], in which he describes the extent to which the discussions and debates that took place at night in Madrid's bars and cafés, "excited by tobacco, coffee and alcohol," were central to the formation of this "generation" of writers and artists (1952, 51). The only women present at such gatherings were prostitutes; thus such an environment was clearly off-limits for "decent" women of the middle and upper classes.

Moreover, Baroja's account reveals the way in which women at this time were excluded, not only from such informal cultural sites as the *tertulia,* but also from centers of formal learning, such as universities and academies. Referring to her metal and enamel work and her successes at exhibitions held in the first decade of the twentieth century, Baroja notes that she did not have the opportunity to receive formal training to enhance her skills: "[M]i vida de señorita bur-

guesa, o acaso mi timidez y falta de arrestos, me impedía desenvolv-
erme, haber ido a una escuela de Bellas Artes, a una academia" [My
life as a bourgeois young woman, or perhaps my timidity and lack of
boldness, impeded my self-development, my going to a school of
Fine Arts, an academy] (1998, 79). Here, once again, there is an element of self-criticism in Baroja's account regarding her failure to
transcend the barriers that excluded her from the educational
arena.

With regard to her intellectual development, Baroja's account reveals that her favorite pastime of reading was an activity considered
inappropriate for women in early twentieth-century Spain. She
notes that she read whenever she could, but almost always furtively,
without her mother's knowledge (1998, 55). That reading and study
were perceived to be not only inappropriate, but also harmful, for
women is confirmed by Carmen Martín Gaite, who affirms that
"caution in education was recommended, as if it were a dangerous
drug that always needed a medical prescription and carefully mea-
sured doses" (2004, 65). Likewise, Mangini affirms that "[r]eading
was thought to rob women of either their faith or their innocence,
and, therefore their virtue" (1995, 103).[4] This notion derives from
the nineteenth-century stereotype of the overly inquisitive woman
or *curieuse*, a figure who, Christine Arkinstall argues, "warns of the
dangers surrounding women's incursions into male-dominated, but
disputed, cultural spaces" (2004, 112).

The above-mentioned characteristics of faith, innocence, and virtue that were perceived to be threatened by intellectual activity are
central traits of the figure of the *ángel del hogar*, the paradigm of
womanhood that dominated late-nineteenth century gender discourse and that constituted the model to which Baroja was expected
to aspire. This model was based on the notion that women were inherently characterized by the above-mentioned qualities, together
with abnegation, submissiveness, and grace, and the presence of
these "natural" virtues in women was evoked to validate the argu-
ment that they were ideally suited to a life of sacrifice in the home.
As such, this ideology sought to justify the exclusion of women from
public life and their restriction to activities centered on the home,
with the domestic space thus posited as "an enclosed space, existing
within the public world, but hidden off from it and inaccessible"
(Aldaraca 1991, 30).

The discourse of the *ángel del hogar* was very much class based, as
is noted by Aldaraca, who confirms that "the ideology of domesticity

is a specifically bourgeois ideology" (1991, 18). As such, this construction of gender cannot be considered in isolation from issues of class. It is, then, an ideology that is certainly pertinent to Baroja, as a middle-class woman living at the turn of the century, and her account reveals the extent to which this model of womanhood was the one that prevailed in her domestic and social environment.

The frustration that Baroja reveals regarding her enclosure in the domestic sphere and her lack of opportunities in the cultural and educational world is accentuated by the author's understanding that education is key for the advancement of women. In 1903, Baroja met and came to admire a number of women who had received a university education and who combined marriage and motherhood with professional endeavors. These women, specifically Carmen Gallardo and María Goyri, both of whom were associated with the Institución Libre de Enseñanza [Institute of Independent Education], were seen by Baroja to represent "el vivo ejemplo de la mujer moderna" [the living example of the modern woman] (Hurtado 1998b, 20).[5] While Baroja does not mention her contact with these women in *Recuerdos,* the importance of her encounter with them is confirmed by her son Julio Caro Baroja. Referring to the relationship between Goyri and her husband, Ramón Menéndez Pidal, which was seen to represent a "rare model of the intellectual marriage in Spain," he remarks that his mother's contact with them "produced great enthusiasm in the young soul of my mother at her twenty or fewer years, who had ideas very much of the era (more those from outside than from inside the country) about the importance of relationships between men and women" (quoted in Rodrigo 2002, 180).

In more general terms, such encounters made Baroja aware of the progressive ideas about women that were beginning to circulate in Spain in the early twentieth century, and the author came to reject definitively the notions that prevailed at that time regarding women's inferiority. Declaring herself to be a feminist, she makes the following affirmation in *Recuerdos:* "Yo creía que si las mujeres, empezando por mí . . . no éramos más inteligentes era por nuestra falta de preparación, por nuestra falta de conocimientos" [I believed that if women, starting with myself . . . were not more intelligent it was due to our lack of education, our lack of knowledge] (1998, 68). Thus despite her criticism of her past self, it is the denial of educational opportunities to women that Baroja highlights as the primary barrier to their intellectual and cultural development.

In this way, the form of feminism that Baroja espouses reflects the focus of the women's movement that developed in Spain in the early twentieth century, which sought to improve women's educational and social rights. Political reform was not a primary concern for the generally conservative feminist groups of the time, an element that is replicated in Baroja's account, in which she does not discuss the specifics of the political changes and gender reforms of the period. Even such an important piece of legislation as the introduction of women's suffrage in 1931 is not discussed in her narrative. In addition, some of Baroja's negative comments regarding women who were active in the literary and political sphere, such as Ernestina de Champourcin, Trudy Graa, and Margarita Nelken, read as very conservative (1998, 103–8). However, while Baroja's attitudes may seem traditional by today's standards, her views must, of course, be considered in relation to her sociohistorical and cultural contexts. Baroja inevitably internalized elements of the education that she received and of her conservative background. We cannot, then, simply transport current thinking to the very different historical context of early twentieth-century Madrid.

Despite her lack of formal educational opportunities, Baroja did realize certain achievements with her craft work in the years prior to her marriage. In fact, in the section of her memoirs in which she narrates the development of her artistic consciousness, Baroja's account reveals her pride at her successes and at the efforts that she did make to construct her own identity, contrary to the domestic roles prescribed for her. She describes objects that she crafted for presentation at Fine Arts exhibitions in 1907 and 1910, noting that she won prizes and gained public recognition for her work: "Los críticos de arte en los periódicos hablaron muy bien de mis obras y hasta se publicó algún retrato mío" [The art critics in the newspapers spoke very highly of my works and even published a picture of me] (1998, 78).

Baroja's choice of metal and enamel work as the outlet for her creativity is particularly anomalous for a woman, with painting being the art form preferred by female artists in the early twentieth century. Her adoption of such a "masculine" art form may be read as a rejection of the artistic models traditionally associated with femininity, as Kirkpatrick has argued: "Baroja's decision to learn an art that utilizes sheet metal, strong acids, and cutting tools . . . could be interpreted as a rejection of the 'feminine' artistic identity in favor of the 'masculine' identity of artisan" (2003, 49–50). However, Kirkpatrick also suggests an alternative interpretation of Baroja's choice of art form, noting that "conversely, the cultivation of a form of craft-work that belonged to the category of the decorative arts could be seen as an extension of the feminine work of embellishing the home, particularly as it was not remunerated" (2003, 50). The fact that Baroja's artwork was not remunerative is significant, for it was only if women's cultural endeavors remained hobbies, rather than "serious" professional undertakings, that they were tolerated by society. This is confirmed by Laura Marcus, who discusses the way in which such a notion operates in relation to women writers. Drawing on Mary Jean Corbett's work on Victorian and Edwardian women's autobiographies (1992), Marcus affirms that "[w]ork, publicity and literary 'professionalism' are radically at odds with 'women's cultural positioning on the inside, at the center of the domestic circle'" (1994, 29).

It is significant that while Baroja highlights her cultural production in the area of metal and enamel work, she does not discuss her vocation as a writer in her memoirs. The publication of Baroja's first works in the 1930s and early 1940s falls within the period covered by her account, which she completed in 1946. She was, moreover, a prolific writer, whose works covered a diversity of genres, including plays, narrative works, film scripts, and works of ethnology and popular customs. Some of Baroja's writings were lost during the Civil War, and many never appeared in print. Hurtado notes that a significant number of unpublished works by Baroja were stored among the family papers where the manuscript of her memoirs was found (1998b, 12). It thus seems unusual that Baroja does not discuss this important element of her life in her text, particularly given the sense of achievement discernible in her recounting of her other cultural pursuits. While the lack of references to her writing may be due to Baroja's awareness of the perceived incompatibility of this activity with a woman's domestic responsibilities, this seems unlikely, given her highlighting of her dissatisfaction with and resistance to such conventional norms in her text. It seems more probable that this significant omission points to the fact that Baroja's manuscript was, indeed, unfinished.

Baroja's cultural interests were particularly incompatible with her role as a married woman, and she affirms that she felt more constrained than ever following her marriage in 1913: "[Y]a no tuve derecho más que a hacer mis labores domésticas y llevar la carga de muchísimas cosas" [Now I had no other right than to carry out my domestic tasks and bear the burden of many things] (1998, 45). Baroja's description of her lack of rights as an individual once she was married accurately reflects the social and legal situation of early twentieth-century Spain, as Scanlon confirms: "Most of the rights that pertained to the single woman disappeared on marriage" (1986, 126). In the brief references that Baroja makes to this period of her life, her account is once again somewhat self-critical, as she writes of what she describes as her lack of intelligence in her relationship with Rafael and of her failure to take the initiative and break free from the ties of the home. She simultaneously notes, however, that such a path was not really open to her, due to her lack of education and financial resources (1998, 45).

The tone of Baroja's writing changes radically when she comes to describe the period that began in 1926, a time that she describes as "de lo más divertido y alegre de mi vida" [among the most enjoyable and happy of my life] (1998, 82), echoing the designation of the 1920s as the *años felices* [happy years]. Baroja's positive memories of these years are indicative of the changing social climate and the new opportunities that this period offered in terms of her cultural and artistic identity. The establishment of the theatrical group El Mirlo Blanco in her brother Ricardo's home brought Baroja into contact with prominent writers and intellectuals, including a number of women who were active on the cultural scene of the day, such as Isabel Oyarzábal de Palencia and Magda Donato. Baroja participated actively in this group that, she affirms, attracted "lo más escogidito de la intelectualidad madrileña" [the most select of the Madrid intelligentsia] (1998, 87).

It is this association with members of Madrid's cultural elite, particularly the above-mentioned women writers, that resulted in Baroja's involvement in the founding of the Lyceum Club in 1926. Baroja presents her involvement in this organization as a positive and stimulating experience that enabled her to meet with other women with similar interests and to participate in the cultural domain, outside the confines of the home. She discusses in some detail the establishment of the Lyceum, recalling the different women involved and the various activities that they organized. This is the only section in Baroja's memoirs in which she refers to the existence of a community of women, who provide support for each other and are able to establish networks of their own. For the most part, her account is one of isolation, with female friends barely mentioned in her memoirs.

Baroja's description of her own role as president of the art section of the Lyceum Club and as the organizer of parts of the Club's lecture program reveals her satisfaction and pride at her involvement in this organization. In fact, throughout Baroja's work, her descriptions of the episodes in her life that did give her access to the cultural world and to an alternative identity to her domestic roles, such as her involvement in fine arts exhibitions and her participation in the Mirlo Blanco and the Lyceum Club, are particularly striking for the intensity and emotion with which these events are narrated. This not only reflects the importance of such opportunities in Baroja's memories of her past, but also emphasizes the fact that these were temporary achievements, standing out as exceptional experiences in a life dominated by gender-based limitations and difficulties.

Moreover, such difficulties continued to face Baroja in the 1920s, with her account revealing the challenges that she faced in combining her responsibilities at the Lyceum Club with her domestic duties. Her husband's inflexibility and lack of support for his wife's endeavors meant that Baroja missed most of the lectures delivered to the Lyceum Club members, despite her role in arranging them, as she was obliged to return home by dinner time (1998, 91). *Recuerdos* thus documents Baroja's constant struggle with the social strictures placed on women of her class, even during the periods of her life when she was involved in the cultural arena.

As political issues came to the forefront of national consciousness during the 1930s, the focus of the Lyceum Club shifted, according to Baroja, who claims that the organization was becoming too political (1998, 103).[6] As a result, Baroja withdrew from the Lyceum in the mid-1930s, indicating her displeasure at the way in which the Club was increasingly dominated by women with left-wing political views.[7]

The question of Baroja's own political positioning is pertinent here. In *Recuerdos*, the author does not express a particular affinity with any political group, gently criticizing both the left and the right at different points in her narrative. Unlike the majority of intellectuals and writers of the day, Baroja was not a supporter of the Republic. Recalling her initial displeasure at its proclamation in April 1931, Baroja makes the following comment with regard to the monarchy: "Me parecía que la monarquía siempre *vestía* más que la república, y que ésta en España había sido una calamidad" [It seemed to me that the monarchy was always more *dressed up* than the Republic, and that the Republic in Spain had been a calamity] (1998, 97; italics in original). Further on, with reference to the years of the Civil War, Baroja affirms that she did not support either side involved in the conflict (1998, 152), and she expresses criticisms of both the Nationalists and the Republicans.

While Baroja's lack of political fervor and activism makes her exceptional in terms of this study, setting her apart quite definitively from Martínez Sierra, León, and Méndez, her lack of involvement in the political sphere and her depiction of the daily struggles that faced her family during this period in fact makes her life story more representative of the experiences of many Spanish women in the 1930s. Although it is true that the changes in gender roles that occurred during the 1920s and the reforms implemented by the Republic, together with the requirements of the war effort, did open up new possibilities for women to participate in traditionally masculine domains, it was nevertheless only a minority of women who actively participated in the political sphere in the 1930s. Moreover, during the Civil War, women in both the Republican and Nationalist zones tended to be mobilized according to conventional constructions of gender, as Helen Graham has argued (1995b, 108). The reality, then, was that the perseverance of traditional gendered norms of conduct impeded widespread changes in women's social roles. That the focus of Baroja's life, and thus that of her memoirs, remained the home and family during the turbulent years of the 1930s and 1940s reflects the reality of this period for many Spanish women, for whom survival was the primary goal.[8]

However, Baroja's lack of political consciousness or strong ideological position is also attributable to her environment. As a woman living in a rigidly traditional context, she would not have been expected to hold political views of her own. Moreover, Baroja would not have had access to models and ideas outside those discussed in her own home, apart, perhaps, from the political conversations held at the Lyceum Club, which, as we have seen, she rejected as inappropriate in that context. Thus the observations made by Baroja in *Recuerdos* with regard to the political situation in her country reflect her education and environment. That Baroja herself did not, or was not expected to, hold political views of her own is confirmed by the focus of her son Pío's text, in which he describes the discussions and disagreements in the household due to his uncles' different opinions. In contrast, he does not make mention of the role of his mother in such conversations, nor does he discuss her political views (Pío Caro Baroja 1996).

Baroja's somewhat ambiguous political positioning may also be attributed to the different views held by members of her family. Baroja's account indicates that her brothers, who served as her main models, had distinct perspectives on the political events of the 1930s. She notes that Ricardo was involved in carrying out political propaganda in 1931 with a group associated with the Ateneo, indicating his connections with groups on the left that sought the establishment of the Republic in Spain.[9] Pío, in contrast, is portrayed as having been highly critical of the founders of the Republic, with Baroja affirming that "Pío no tenía ninguna simpatía y menos confianza en la capacidad de los padres de la República y no se recataba de decirlo" [Pío had no sympathy for and less confidence in the capabilities of the fathers of the Republic and he did not shrink from saying so] (1998, 100).[10] Similarly, in the postwar period, Baroja's brothers adopted different stances regarding the political situation in Spain and Europe. While Pío is described in Baroja's son Pío's account as feeling "a profound disgust for triumphant Spain," as well as for Hitler and Mussolini (Pío Caro Baroja 1996, 82), and is said to have hoped for the victory of the Allies in the Second World War, Pío Caro Baroja notes the opposing position held by his other uncle: "Ricardo, paradoxically, was a Germanophile in those years, because he believed in an Aryan paganism, and that Hitler would sweep Europe clean of Christian and Catholic blights and decay" (1996, 83). These conflicting views were, then, those that influenced Baroja, and perhaps such diversity of opinion within her own family further contributed to the fact that Baroja does not present political events from any fixed ideological stance in *Recuerdos*.

Baroja's account of the years of the Civil War is not, then, politically motivated; rather, she recounts the events of the war as she experienced them in the Basque Country, narrating the consequences of the conflict on her own family. Baroja was already in Vera, together with her sons and brothers, when the war broke out in July 1936, but Rafael was still in Madrid, and was to remain separated from the rest of the family for the duration of the war. Due to the relative isolation of their country house, Baroja notes that in the early stages of the war "vivíamos en gran inconsciencia" [we lived in great unawareness] (1998, 156). However, as news reached them of the events taking place in their region and throughout the country, the family became more aware of the gravity of the situation. Baroja recalls the news of the raids on houses in the area and the intense bombing campaign centered on the region, which soon became Nationalist-controlled territory.[11] In the aftermath of the bombings and at a time when Vera was close to the frontline, Baroja recounts her role assisting with tending to the wounded at a temporary hospital set up in the village (1998, 162–68). Pío managed to escape to France at this time, although he did return to Vera to visit the family once during the war, in 1938.

As it became apparent that the war might continue for some time, the family's lack of financial resources and support in Vera meant that they had to become self-sufficient in order to survive. They therefore grew crops and kept animals in the fields surrounding the house, and Baroja's account of this period reveals her resourcefulness in this regard: "Yo me leí toda la literatura enciclopédica sobre la cría de gallinas, cerdos, conejos, etcétera, así que mi cultura se hizo muy vasta y llegué incluso a darme importancia con los labriegos" [I read up on all the encyclopedic literature about the raising of chickens, pigs, rabbits, etcetera, so that my education became very vast and even came to give me an importance among the farm hands] (1998, 175). However, Baroja simultaneously communicates the hardship of these years, a reality that is likewise depicted in Pío Caro Baroja's portrait of the period: "They were difficult years of economic penury, which [my mother] confronted with enormous fortitude, working in the garden and the fields like a peasant. Her agile and fine hands, accustomed to lace making and to playing the Sonatas of Mozart, became hard and cracked, but she supported her family" (1996, 199). The increasing desperation of the family as the war continued is also clear in Baroja's work, as she affirms that they were becoming physically weaker as time passed and would not have survived had the war lasted another year (1998, 183).

While Baroja's description of the war years thus emphasizes the difficulties that she encountered during this period of her life, she also expresses a sense of pride regarding the way that she dealt with the additional responsibilities that she faced. In a sense, Baroja's portrayal of her lived experiences during the years of the Spanish Civil War evokes something of the spirit of the "Generation of 1898" with which the writer identified, as she focuses on the way in which her daily activities brought her in touch with nature and the realities of life. Thus while Baroja's account of these years does not focus on any artistic or intellectual activities, her depiction of her lived experiences reinforces her association with the "generation" to which she refers in the title of her work.

Despite her disconnection from the cultural world at this time, Baroja did write during the war years, using this activity as a means of seeking some relief from the difficulties of daily life during the years of the conflict. This was the period in which she wrote her work of fiction for children entitled *Martinito, el de la Casa Grande* (1942), a tale that she composed to comfort her sons during the war, as Pío Caro Baroja has confirmed (1996, 199). Furthermore, Baroja wrote other works of fiction during this period, texts that were never published, as well as a number of articles for the magazine *Mujer* (Hurtado 1998b, 34). Once again, Baroja silences this aspect of her activity in her memoirs, making no reference to her literary production of the war period.

When the Civil War ended, Baroja and her family returned to Madrid, where they were reunited with Rafael. Both their former home and their publishing company had been destroyed during the war, along with most of their possessions, and the continuing hardships that they faced during the period immediately following the conflict is highlighted in Baroja's work. It is during this period, between 1939 and 1946, that Baroja wrote her memoirs, and her proximity to the events that she recounts, particularly those of the 1930s and 1940s, inevitably affects her portrayal of these years. She does not write from the different perspective that distance from the events recalled can bring; rather, Baroja wrote her memoirs in the midst of the so-called *años de hambre* [years of hunger] of the 1940s, a period characterized by "la horrible carestía de la vida" [the horrible scarcities of life] as she notes (1998, 209). Baroja's depiction of the harsh economic conditions of the decade following the war is confirmed by Martín Gaite's description of these years: "It is well known that those so-called triumphal years were characterized by great economic penury, severe drought, low agricultural wages, lack of housing for people who moved from the country to the city, and poor public service" (2004, 23).[12]

Baroja's proximity to these events as she writes her memoirs thus gives her a different kind of access to the past that she recalls and recounts. While this has implications for the memory process, potentially resulting in a less problematic divide between the self that experienced the events of the 1930s and 1940s and the remembering self, this should not be read as an indication that Baroja's account is inherently more representative of the "truth" than are memory texts written some decades after the events took place. Autobiographical writing always involves the narrative reconstruction of a life history, a process that provides an opportunity for the rereading of the past from the standpoint of the present, regardless of the duration of the intervening period.

The fact that sections of Baroja's account narrate events of the author's very recent past also serves to further separate her account from traditional masculinist conceptions of autobiographical writing, which advocate a certain aloofness on the part of the writing subject. George Gusdorf, for example, maintains that autobiography "requires a man to take a distance with regard to himself in order to reconstitute himself in the focus of his special unity and identity across time" (1980, 35). Such distance is arguably not achieved in Baroja's text, nor does her work articulate a unity in terms of the identity of the writing self.

While in general Baroja reflects little on the memory process in *Recuerdos,* she does recognize the subjective nature of such writing. Affirming that she seeks to provide an accurate representation of herself and her past, she simultaneously notes that such a description will inevitably be written from her own personal point of view (1998, 48). Baroja also indicates an awareness of the extent to which autobiographical writing is an inherently self-centered form: "[D]ejaremos aquí, sobre el papel, abierto el grifo de la egolatría más desenfrenada, que salga a toda llave el YO más estruendoso" [We will leave here, on paper, the tap opened on the most unbridled self-glorification, which gushes out with full force the most thunderous I] (1998, 47). Such a focus on the self is incompatible with conventional definitions of femininity, with pervasive stereotypes constructing the "true" woman as modest and self-effacing. As such, the inherently self-assertive and self-revealing nature of autobiographical writing has traditionally been considered unseemly for women. In fact, as Sidonie Smith argues, according to patriarchal ideology "woman has no 'autobiographical self' in the sense that man does . . . she has no 'public' story to tell" (1987, 50).

Baroja appears to recognize that, by writing her memoirs and criticizing her family and environment, she contravenes the norms of abnegation and submissiveness that characterize formulations of womanhood in her sociohistorical context, norms that have defined her own existence for so many years. In her case, the autobiographical process involves the act of what Norine Voss describes as "saying the unsayable" (1986, 229–30): that is, expressing emotions such as anger and resentment that have long been considered taboo for women. Accustomed to subordinating the demands of the self to those of others, through her writing Baroja now seeks to express herself as she has never been permitted to do, focusing on herself as the subject of her narrative: "[M]e voy a hartar de escribir sobre mis pensamientos, mis ideas, mi persona. Puede que hasta adornarme un poco" [I shall become fed up with writing about my thoughts, my ideas, my persona. Maybe to the point of embellishing myself a little] (1998, 47). Baroja thus also notes here that while she seeks to provide an accurate account of her self and past, her writing may contain the distortions and omissions characteristic of memory writing.[13]

In addition, the split between the past and present selves inherent to autobiography is signaled by Baroja, who notes that the past self that she represents in *Recuerdos* is at times unfamiliar to her: "A veces me reconozco y a veces me parece que se trata de una persona que yo hace años conocí" [Sometimes I recognize myself and sometimes it seems to me that it is a person whom I met years ago] (1998, 43). Throughout much of her text, Baroja is highly critical of this autobiographical persona, making repeated references to what she considers to be weaknesses in her own character that led her to expect too much from life and thus resulted in her unhappiness. She recalls herself, for example, as "una casada defraudada por el romanticismo, egoísta, sin duda, por haber pedido a la vida más de lo que en general suele otorgar" [a married woman disappointed by romanticism, selfish, without doubt, for having asked of life more than it generally gives] (1998, 43). The unhappiness and resentment from which Baroja suffered for much of her life are thus attributed in her account to both the environment in which she lived and her own personality, as the following affirmation reveals: "De lo que estoy segura es que no podré dar a mis recuerdos la tristeza, la nostalgia y el aburrimiento que he padecido durante toda mi vida, sin duda debido a mi carácter y también al medio en que he vivido" [What I am sure of is that I will not be able to give my memories the sadness, nostalgia, and boredom from which I have suffered throughout my life, doubtless due to my character and also to the environment in which I have lived] (1998, 48). Despite her declarations that she herself is partly responsible for the resentment that she feels regarding the monotony of her life, Baroja's text leaves the reader in no doubt that it is the latter factor that is the real cause of her unhappiness.

While contemporary critics such as Mangini (2001) and Kirkpatrick (2003) concur that it was undeniably the rigid environment in which Baroja lived that prevented her from realizing her aspirations, more traditional writers fail to acknowledge the overwhelming effects of social conditioning on Baroja's life. Miguel Pérez Ferrero, for example, referring to Baroja, maintains that "she lacked the tenacity that was markedly evident in both Pío and Ricardo" (1972, 310), suggesting that it is a lack of determination on Baroja's part that limited her achievements in comparison with those of her highly successful brothers. Writer Mercedes Formica, herself a defender of equal legal rights for women, comments that Baroja "knew how to harmonize her multiple intellectual gifts with family life" (1998, 95). While going on to note Baroja's many cultural talents and her concern for the role of women in society, Formica writes that the author "forgot her own vocations so that her family could develop those that they felt" (1998, 102), thus suggesting that the subordination of her own interests was a conscious and voluntary choice made by Baroja, rather than a reality imposed on her by social norms.

Carmen Baroja's *Recuerdos de una mujer de la generación del 98* is a narrative that reveals the pervasive feminine stereotypes that dominated life for women of her social class in late nineteenth- and early twentieth-century Spain. As a member of a prominent literary family, with two brothers who belonged to Madrid's cultural elite at the turn of the century, Baroja may appear to have had privileged access to the cultural world. However, if, in a limited sense, she was able to operate within the literary and cultural arena of her time, Baroja's work makes it clear that she was simultaneously very much on the periphery of its legitimating boundaries. Characterized by qualifications and self-criticism, Baroja's autobiography is, nevertheless, an exploration of self-inscription and subjectivity that documents the strong pressures on women to fulfill cultural expectations. Mapping out an identity defined largely by exclusion, Baroja produces a self-reflective account that highlights her achievements in her chosen art form of metal and enamel work and her participation in cultural endeavors in the 1920s, despite the overwhelming obstacles that limited her creativity and freedom.

3

María Martínez Sierra (1874–1974), *Una mujer por caminos de España* and *Gregorio y yo:* Writing, Politics, and Feminism

MARÍA MARTÍNEZ SIERRA, BORN MARÍA DE LA O LEJÁRRAGA, WAS ONE OF the most important feminist political figures of early twentieth-century Spain, as well as one of the most prolific and successful women writers of the period. As an educated woman who participated not only in the cultural sphere, writing and publishing, but also in the political arena as an orator and parliamentary representative for the Spanish Socialist Party, Martínez Sierra defied the gendered norms of the society in which she lived. A complex figure, she published most of her works under her husband's name, thus choosing to remain on the periphery of the public literary arena. At the same time, she adopted a prominent role in the political sphere and vindicated the rights of women. It is Martínez Sierra's representation of these different facets of her past in her two autobiographical texts, *Una mujer por caminos de España* and *Gregorio y yo,* that will be examined in this chapter.

Martínez Sierra was born in La Rioja in 1874, but spent most of her childhood and adolescence in Madrid, after her family moved to the capital in 1880. Unlike many of her contemporaries, she received a liberal upbringing and an education that prepared her for a future career, thanks to the progressive ideals held by her parents. Educated at home by her mother until the age of thirteen, she went on to study at the Asociación de Enseñanza de la Mujer [Association for the Education of Women], later training to be a primary school teacher at the Teacher's Training College in Madrid. In 1895 Martínez Sierra took up her first position as a teacher, and it was her early teaching experiences in a poor area of Madrid that alerted her to the extreme poverty that existed in Spain at the time: "[C]onocí . . . a través de su chiquillería, la miseria negra del proletariado madrileño de entonces" [Through their children, I became aware of the terrible poverty of the Madrid proletariat of those times] (1989, 81). While she had previously been aware of class differences, noting the struggle of her own middle-class family to make ends meet on the doctor's salary earned by her father, Martínez Sierra notes that she had never appreciated the extent of such divisions and had, as a child, assumed these to be a part of the natural order: "Se nace en casa pobre o en familia pudiente o de la clase media, como se nace rubio o moreno, enfermo o sano" [One is born into a poor household or into a well-to-do or middle-class family in the same way one is born blond or brunette, ill or healthy] (1989, 79). It is this realization of the extreme poverty in which many Spaniards lived to which the author attributes her identification with the socialist ideology: "[H]e venido al socialismo por mera realización de la miseria ambiente" [I have come to socialism simply through awareness of the poverty around me] (1989, 82).

It was not, however, until some years later that political activity became the focus of Martínez Sierra's life. For the first decades of the twentieth century, teaching and writing were the two activities to which she dedicated her time and energy. Among her first publications were a volume of short stories for children, published under the title *Cuentos breves: Lecturas recreativas para niños* [Short Tales: Recreational Readings for Children] (1899),[1] and a volume entitled *El poema del trabajo* [Labor's Poem] (1898). This latter text was published under the name of her future husband, Gregorio Martínez Sierra (1881–1947), with whom she had developed a close friendship in 1897. The couple married in 1900, and from that time the numerous dramatic and narrative works and essays written by María Martínez Sierra were published under Gregorio's name, in what she describes as a "collaboration" between them.[2]

The moderate success of their plays, novels, and short stories in these early years allowed Martínez Sierra to resign from her teaching position in 1907 in order to dedicate herself fully to writing. Her literary production during this period was prolific: between 1907 and 1911, for example, she wrote, among other works, some sixteen plays, with a similar number appearing between 1911 and 1915. From 1911, the literary fame of "Gregorio Martínez Sierra" was secure, due to the tremendous success of the play *Canción de cuna* [Cradle Song] (1911). In addition to writing, between 1903 and 1904 Martínez Sierra and Gregorio, together with three of their contemporaries, produced the journal *Helios.* Although short-lived, this was one of the most important Modernist publications of the period, and has been described as "a cultural reference point for the Madrid of that era" (Romero Marín 2000, 562). Some years later, María and Gregorio Martínez Sierra produced another journal, *Renacimiento,* which took its title from the Catalan term *Renaixença* [Renaissance]: the name of both the nineteenth-century movement that celebrated the revival of Catalan literature and culture and also that of an earlier Catalan Modernist publication (Bretz 2001, 33).[3]

It was in the second decade of the twentieth century that Martínez Sierra produced her first feminist writings, also published under Gregorio's name. In total, "Gregorio Martínez Sierra" published four volumes of epistolary essays on feminism between 1916 and 1932.[4] In addition, in 1931 Martínez Sierra published under her own name *La mujer española ante la república* [The Spanish Woman and the Republic] (1931), a collection of essays in which she espouses the social and legal rights of women. In contrast to many of her contemporaries who eschewed the label of "feminist," Martínez Sierra makes the following categorical affirmation regarding her positioning vis-à-vis feminism: "He sido, soy y seré feminista" [I have been, I am and I shall be a feminist] (1989, 55). Furthermore, in her essays she encourages the women whom she addresses to adopt feminist stances, urging them to disregard the stigma of the feminist label: "Y no se avergüencen ustedes de la pelea, no les dé rumor proclamarse de una vez para siempre feministas. Están ustedes obligadas a serlo por ley de naturaleza. Una mujer que no fuese feminista sería un absurdo tan grande como un militar que no fuese militarista o como un rey que no fuese monárquico" [And do not be ashamed of the fight, do not be embarrassed to declare yourselves feminists once and for all. You are obliged by nature to be feminists. A woman who was not a feminist would be as ridiculous as a military man who was not militarist or a king who was not a monarchist] (quoted in Blanco 2003, 96).[5]

Martínez Sierra's identification with the concerns of the nascent feminist movement in Spain are also evidenced by her participation in a number of the women's groups that emerged during this period. Among these is the Unión de Mujeres de España [Union of Spanish Women], of which Martínez Sierra became secretary; this was the Spanish branch of the International Woman Suffrage Alliance. She later participated in the founding of the Lyceum Club, serving as the Club's librarian, and was involved with the Club from 1926 to 1930. Martínez Sierra then became the founding president of the Asociación Femenina de Educación Cívica [Feminine Association for Civic Education], an organization that sought to disseminate feminist ideas among women of the middle classes. Furthermore, she became a prominent public speaker on issues related to women's rights, giving lectures at the *Ateneo* in Madrid during the 1920s.

During this period, Martínez Sierra spent a significant amount of time at the house she had had built in Cagnes-sur-Mer (France), seeking some respite from the frenetic pace of her life in Madrid and from the painful reality of Gregorio's relationship with actress Catalina Bárcena, for whom he left his wife in 1922 after Bárcena gave birth to his child. Despite Gregorio's decision to leave her, and his absence from Spain as he traveled to Hollywood in search of further theatrical opportunities, Martínez Sierra nevertheless continued to write plays for him, while simultaneously championing the rights of women in her writings and speeches. The complexities of the author's positioning in this respect will be discussed in the ensuing analysis.

It was with the advent of the Second Republic that Martínez Sierra came to dedicate herself fully to politics, ending three decades of literary production in the name of Gregorio Martínez Sierra. In the public arena of politics, Martínez Sierra continued to give numerous speeches and lectures promoting the legal and social rights of women, and she became more involved in the Spanish Socialist Party, the PSOE (Partido Socialista Obrero Español) [Spanish Socialist Workers' Party]. In 1933 she was elected to Parliament as the party's representative for Granada. She was extremely active in this role, both in terms of her participation in parliamentary debates and her campaigning in different areas of Spain for social and legal reform to put an end to the injustices of the social and political systems in place in her country.

Martínez Sierra did not, however, complete her parliamentary term, resigning in 1934 in protest at the government's repression of the Asturian miners. This resignation did not signal the end of her political activism. Rather, she continued campaigning, now on behalf of the Organización Pro Infancia Obrero [Organization for Working Class Children].[6] Shortly after the outbreak of the Civil War, the Republican government appointed Martínez Sierra as its commercial attaché in Switzerland, and in 1937 she represented Spain at an international labor conference in Geneva. When she left her posting in Switzerland in 1938, Martínez Sierra settled in her house in Nice. She lived in France until 1950, when she moved to the United States and Mexico, before settling in Buenos Aires in 1953, where she resided until her death in 1974. During her years of exile, Martínez Sierra continued to write and to produce translations. It is at the beginning of her exile in the Americas that her two autobiographical texts were first published, although these did not appear in her homeland for many years.

Works written by "Gregorio Martínez Sierra" are particularly important in the context of the Spanish literary scene of the early twentieth century, due both to the fact that their production spanned more than three decades and also to the tremendous success of many of these works. It was primarily "Gregorio Martínez Sierra's" plays that elicited critical acclaim, many of which were staged in Madrid's best theaters. In general, their poetry, novels, and short stories received less public and critical praise. In addition, essays and speeches produced by "Gregorio Martínez Sierra" were very important in the context of the debate on the "woman question" that was taking place during this period.[7] The literary production of "Gregorio Martínez Sierra" thus occupied a central place in the Spanish literary landscape of the day, despite the fact that María Martínez Sierra herself chose to live on the margins of the literary scene.

The literary production of "Gregorio Martínez Sierra" ceased around the time that Martínez Sierra became involved in the political arena. Apart from some political writings, it was not until the 1950s that further texts by Martínez Sierra were published, with the appearance of her two autobiographical texts that she wrote during the 1930s and 1940s. The first of these, *Una mujer por caminos de España,* first published in Buenos Aires in 1952, recounts her political role as a socialist, a feminist, and a Parliamentarian, working to defend the ideals of the Second Republic. Published the following year in Mexico City, Martínez Sierra's second autobiographical work, *Gregorio y yo: Medio siglo de colaboración,* focuses on aspects of the author's personal and literary history. The question of Martínez Sierra's decision to divide her life story into two separate texts is central to the ensuing analysis.

Much of the scholarly work produced to date on María Martínez Sierra has tended to focus on the question of what the author herself termed the "collaboration" between herself and her husband.[8] Gregorio confirmed that his literary works had been written in collaboration with his wife in a document that was among his official papers when he died in 1947: "I declare for legal purposes that all my works are written in collaboration with my wife" (quoted in Lafitte 1964, 242). Despite this affirmation, for some decades after Gregorio's death, some critics continued to deny María Martínez Sierra's role. Federico Carlos Sainz de Robles, for example, stated categorically in his 1971 study that there was no doubt that Gregorio Martínez Sierra was "the sole author of countless and admirable dramatic works, and of admirable novels and essays" (1971, 107). The inaccuracy of this affirmation is, however, now widely accepted by scholars, with Patricia O'Connor's study (1977) conclusively demonstrating that the works published under Gregorio's name were actually written by his wife.

Despite the fact that he was not the author of the numerous literary works that secured his fame, the importance of Gregorio Martínez Sierra as a prominent member of the cultural elite of early twentieth-century Madrid should not be overlooked. A highly successful stage director and manager in the theatre industry, Gregorio managed the famous Eslava Theater from 1916 to 1926 and established several theater companies during his career. Critics have described Gregorio as "the greatest artistic director the Spanish theatre has known" (quoted in Reyero Hermosilla 1980, 4) and "one of the pioneers of the Spanish theatrical scene of the twentieth century" (Checa Puerta 1992, 126).[9] In addition, Gregorio was the founder of a number of important Modernist literary journals and publishing houses, activities in which María Martínez Sierra also participated.

While Antonina Rodrigo's analysis characterizes Gregorio as a "predator" and Martínez Sierra as a victim of her husband, described as his "slave" (1994, 175), it is important to bear in mind that Martínez Sierra chose to publish under her husband's name. The author emphasizes this point in *Gregorio y yo,* where she affirms that the name of "Gregorio Martínez Sierra" was "adoptado voluntariamente como cifra de nuestra común ilusión juvenil" [voluntarily adopted as the monogram of our joint youthful illusion] (2000, 97). This was not, then, an anonymity imposed on Martínez Sierra by her husband, although her comment does signal that there was perhaps an element of youthful romanticism in this decision. It is the voluntary aspect of Martínez Sierra's decision, not only to publish under Gregorio's name but also to maintain the myth of joint authorship after the couple's separation and after her husband's death, that is emphasized by Alda Blanco in her insightful discussions of Martínez Sierra's work. Blanco contends that Martínez Sierra's decision to preserve her anonymity was a consciously strategic act on her part to use his name as a pseudonym, in order to be able to participate in a decidedly masculine literary scene. Proposing a rereading of this aspect of the author's life, Blanco observes that "[p]odríamos, entonces, reescenificar su matrimonio y anonimato como un espacio no de opresión y explotación, sino más bien de libertad que le permitió desarrollar la vocación que tanto le apasionaba sin tener que preocuparse del necio qué dirán" [we could, then, restage her marriage and anonymity as a space not of oppression and exploitation, but rather of freedom, which enabled her to develop the vocation about which she was so passionate without having to worry about becoming the butt of idiotic gossip] (2000, 26).

The social stigma attached to women writers in the sociohistorical context to which Blanco refers is signaled by Martínez Sierra herself in *Gregorio y yo* as a factor in her decision to write under Gregorio's name: "[N]o quería empañar la limpieza de mi nombre con la dudosa fama que en aquella época caía como sambenito casi deshonroso sobre toda mujer 'literata'" [I did not wish to stain my good name with the dubious fame which in those days hung almost like a label of dishonor on every woman of letters] (2000, 76). In this way, Martínez Sierra indicates that the use of her husband's name was a means of protecting her social standing and avoiding public criticism, evoking Carolyn Heilbrun's observation that "anonymity eases women's pains, alleviates the anxiety about the appropriateness of gender" (1989, 40). Martínez Sierra's deployment of Gregorio's name as a pseudonym was a particularly effective strategy as regards the reception of her feminist essays. Given that matters pertaining to social or political theory were considered to be masculine domains, these writings certainly had a greater status if they were perceived to be penned by a man, as well as suggesting a more objective positioning vis-à-vis feminism. As Sidonie Smith has affirmed with regard to women autobiographers' use of male pseudonyms, "[t]hey understand that a statement or a story will receive a different ideological interpretation if attributed to a man or to a woman" (1987, 49).

A further important consideration here relates to the question of genre and the fact that much of Martínez Sierra's literary production was written for the stage. While it was considered inappropriate for women to participate in literary endeavors per se, the public nature of the theatrical world meant that drama was particularly incompatible with conventional constructions of femininity. The difficulties faced by female playwrights in this era are signaled by

Nieva de la Paz, who notes that "in the case of female playwrights it is necessary to overcome new obstacles, given that it was much more difficult to enter the complex circuits of theatrical dissemination" (1998, 161). The playwright's role extended well beyond the writing of the literary work, with the author attending rehearsals and premieres of his or her plays and interacting with the public and critics. That Gregorio, as the supposed author of their plays, adopted this public role is made explicit by Martínez Sierra in her description of the premiere of *Canción de cuna:* "Mi compañero andaba entre bastidores, como es costumbre, animando a los intérpretes, o más bien compartiendo con ellos el pánico de la primera representación; yo, en el palco, me limitaba a presenciar el alumbramiento con no menos terror, debo confesarlo" [My partner went into the wings, as is customary, encouraging the actors, or rather sharing with them the panic of the first night; I, in the stalls, limited myself to witnessing the birth with, I must confess, no less terror] (2000, 352). For Martínez Sierra, then, the anonymity provided by Gregorio's name enabled her to avoid the opprobrium that her transgressive participation in the public arena of the theater would undoubtedly have created. Given such an unreceptive environment, it is not surprising that there were far fewer women playwrights active in late nineteenth and early twentieth-century Spain than there were female poets and novelists.

In addition to the factors outlined above, Martínez Sierra attributes her decision to write under her husband's name to her family's unenthusiastic reception of her first publication—the author recalls that "[e]l acontecimiento no despertó entusiasmo ni ocasionó celebración alguna" [the event occasioned neither enthusiasm nor any celebration whatsoever] (2000, 75)—as well as to her youth and romanticism (2000, 76). This latter reason is, Rodrigo maintains, the overriding reason for Martínez Sierra's decision, with this critic affirming that "the other reasons are pretexts, the true motivation for her total submission and renunciation in favor of Gregorio was love" (1994, 58). However, such a reading of Martínez Sierra's stance does not fully take into account the complexities of the social and literary contexts in which the author operated and neglects the other factors that contributed to her adoption of Gregorio's name as a pseudonym.

While Martínez Sierra was undoubtedly aware of the gendered nature of the literary world, she does not focus in her life-writing on the place of women intellectuals on the cultural scene in early twentieth-century Madrid, nor does she depict the limitations placed on women in this sphere as affecting her personally. Unlike some of her contemporaries who express resentment at their exclusion from key sites of intellectual practice, Martínez Sierra implies that she participated as fully as she wished in the literary scene of the day, avoiding a more public, integral role by choice. While Martínez Sierra notes, for example, that she did not attend the literary *tertulias* of the time, gatherings that were without doubt male-dominated, she does not suggest that this is due to restrictions placed on her as a woman, implying, rather, that it was a matter of personal choice: "No he sido nunca noctámbula, y de día tenía harto quehacer; así es que nunca he frecuentado cenáculos literarios" [I have never been one to go out at night, and during the day I had a lot to do; so I have never frequented literary gatherings] (2000, 90).

Moreover, although she chose to remain officially on the periphery of the cultural arena, Martínez Sierra's relationship with Gregorio gave her a form of access to the literary center. Gregorio participated in the *tertulias* that were central to the shaping of Modernist culture during this period, and he established valuable connections with influential figures in the literary world in early twentieth-century Madrid. Martínez Sierra's account recognizes that her relationship with Gregorio and the networks to which he had access were of benefit to her, as it was his influence and name that allowed her works to be published and staged. Martínez Sierra, then, does not question the exclusionary and masculinist nature of the intellectual scene, a domain in which she presents herself as participating together with well-known figures of Madrid's male literary elite of the period.

In *Gregorio y yo*, Martínez Sierra aligns herself with the Generation of 1898, invoking the *nosotros* [we] form with reference to this group: "Se ha dado en llamar 'generación del 98' al grupo de escritores que empezamos a emborronar papel en los últimos años del siglo XIX" [We group of writers who began to scribble on paper in the last years of the nineteenth century have come to be called the "Generation of 1898"] (2000, 59). She likewise expresses some of the sentiments and preoccupations that characterized writings by well-known figures of this "generation," discussing the reaction of herself and her contemporaries to the "disaster" of 1898 and the effect that it had on their feelings toward their *patria* [homeland] (2000, 62–64). Martínez Sierra goes on to note the resulting devaluation of things Spanish: "Para los españoles de los primeros años del siglo XX todo lo de fuera parecía bueno por contraste con el atraso de dentro de casa" [For Spaniards of the first years of the twentieth century everything from outside seemed good in contrast with the backwardness of home] (2000, 65). The prestige attributed during this period to products, ideas, and influences from outside Spain is similarly noted by historians, who indicate the perceived inferiority of Spain in comparison with its European neighbors. Such an attitude was, moreover, characteristic of the vision held by many of the writers of the "Generation of 1898," who, José Luis Comellas affirms, regarded their country as "backward, ignorant, coarse, useless, vulgar, sanctimonious in the worst sense of the word, and more African than European" (2002, 71). Martínez Sierra thus replicates a number of the concerns expressed by this canonical group of writers.

Critics place Martínez Sierra and the works of "Gregorio Martínez Sierra" firmly within the Modernist movement that dominated the literary scene of turn-of-the-century Spain. Ricardo Gullón, for example, affirms that "it is impossible to write a history of Spanish literary Modernism" (1961, 9) without taking into account the works of "Gregorio Martínez Sierra," and Kirkpatrick argues that Martínez Sierra had a place "in the very nucleus of Spanish Modernism" (2003, 132). This alignment of Martínez Sierra with Modernism does not necessarily preclude the identification of this writer with the "Generation of 1898," a movement that, as previously noted, can be said to represent an early Modernism. Indeed, these movements and the "generations" traditionally associated with them— those of 1898, 1914, 1927, and so on—are overlapping and interacted, as scholars such as Bretz (2001) and Santiáñez (2004) have argued. In fact, recent criticism includes works produced by canonical figures of the "Generation of 1898," such as Valle-Inclán, Unamuno, Ganivet, and Azorín, under the Modernist label, thus negating the traditional division between the movements.

However, Martínez Sierra herself emphatically rejects any association of the literary works of "Gregorio Martínez Sierra" with Modernism, affirming that this inaccurate label made it difficult for them to have their works staged in the early days of their literary career. Contrary to the branding of their works as Modernist, Martínez Sierra contends that all of their literary production was unquestionably realist in nature: "[El cuento e]ra 'realista' como toda nuestra producción literaria, ya que, a pesar del sambenito de modernistas, soñadores y amerengados que ha echado sobre nuestros hombros la crítica, a veces malévola, hasta nuestras más etéreas fantasías tienen su esqueleto en la pura . . . realidad" [The story was "realist," like all our literary production, for in spite of the defamatory label of modernists and affected dreamers that the critics have placed on our shoulders, sometimes with malevolence, even our most ethereal fantasies have their basis in pure . . . reality] (2000, 96). By aligning their works in this way with the "Generation of 1898" but in contrast with Modernism, Martínez Sierra may be seen to replicate the retrospective differentiation of these two groups and the concomitant privileging of the former over the latter, a split that was discussed in chapter 1. This division resulted in the work of the "Generation of 1898" coming to be viewed as more profound and truly "Spanish" writing, while Modernism was dismissed as superficial and unrealistic.[10]

However, Martínez Sierra's rejection of the Modernist label may also be attributable to the negative portrayals of this literary mode that circulated in late nineteenth-century Spain. There was much debate over the literary merit of works produced by the young, "modern" writers of the period, designated the *gente nueva* [newcomers] by critics. The use of this term is explained by Dobón: "The appellation of *gente nueva* was popularized in the late 1890s and, although it designates young writers who introduce revolutionary ideas into the end-of-century literary world, above all it designates the modernists" (1996, 61n5). In a series of articles published in 1897, Leopoldo Alas (Clarín) criticized this group, affirming in one article that among them "I see neither truly inspired lyric poets nor dramatists of a really literary nature, nor novelists, nor art critics" (1897). While the writers and artists deemed to belong to such a group also had their supporters, it is perhaps unsurprising that Martínez Sierra was reluctant to be aligned with such a controversial movement.

Notwithstanding Martínez Sierra's affirmations to the contrary, a further factor that aligns this writer and her husband with Modernism is their involvement in the production of the literary journal *Helios*. This publication, of which fourteen issues were published between April 1903 and May 1904, was described by Ricardo Gullón as "the best journal of Modernism" (1961, 14), although Martínez Sierra herself contends that Gregorio conceived it as "moderna y no modernista" [modern and not Modernist] (2000, 226). *Helios* was a project developed by María and Gregorio Martínez Sierra, together with Juan Ramón Jiménez, Pedro González Blanco, and Ramón

Pérez de Ayala, aimed at providing a publication outlet for both established and emerging writers. In her account of this joint venture in *Gregorio y yo*, Martínez Sierra highlights her integration in the otherwise all-male editorial team. Using the inclusive *nosotros* form, Martínez Sierra explains that they each contributed financially to cover the paper and printing costs of the publication, and that they all collaborated in the different editorial tasks, noting that "[n]osotros cinco hacíamos de todo" [we five did everything] (2000, 227). Martínez Sierra thus depicts herself as working alongside her male contemporaries on equal terms, without suggesting that her role in what was clearly a man's world might be anomalous. The male-dominated nature of the literary scene is, in fact, revealed by Martínez Sierra's own account, in which she lists some of the most important contributors to *Helios,* among whom she includes only one woman, Emilia Pardo Bazán. While writings by Martínez Sierra herself were included in the publication, these appeared, of course, under Gregorio's name.

In direct contrast to Martínez Sierra's chosen anonymity in the literary world is her visibility as a politician and a feminist in the public sphere of politics. Martínez Sierra had a more visible public and political profile than did any of the other writers examined in this book. Although León's important work during the years of the Republic did give her some prominence, Martínez Sierra's involvement in the formal political sphere made her a more public figure. Martínez Sierra's decision to divide her life story into two separate texts suggests a resistance on the part of the author to bring together the different facets of her past self in her writing. The public self of socialist campaigner and feminist activist that is the subject of *Una mujer* is set apart from the private self of wife, collaborator, and writer that is the focus of *Gregorio y yo*. While the role of writer is not typically a private identity, it is in the case of Martínez Sierra, due to her use of Gregorio's name as a pseudonym that ensured her anonymity.

Martínez Sierra's desire to have at least part of her life story published in Spain was perhaps a factor in her division of her past into two texts. While the author had anticipated that *Una mujer* would not be published in her homeland due to the strict censorship restrictions put in place by the Franco regime, she had intended to publish *Gregorio y yo* there. Martínez Sierra did not expect the latter text to be particularly controversial, noting that "en él no se trata más que de vida literaria sin política ni religión" [it deals with nothing more than literary life, without politics or religion] (quoted in Blanco 2000, 13). She did not appear to understand fully the extent to which her political roles during the years of the Republic positioned her as an "enemy," according to the regime. As a woman who had been a propagandist and a member of Parliament for the Socialist Party, as well as a feminist activist and a Republican representative abroad during the war years, Martínez Sierra was very much seen as representative of the "anti-España" [anti-Spain] constructed and abhorred by the Franco regime. This "anti-España," as Republican Spain was designated, was described by Francoist Rafael Gil Serrano in the following terms: "The destructive Spain, the damaging Spain, . . . the black Spain, the horror Spain, the monstrous Spain" (quoted in Rodríguez Puértolas 1987, 1001). Deemed to form part of such a group, it is hardly surprising that Martínez Sierra's life-writing should have been considered inappropriate for publication in Francoist Spain. The official versions of history and collective memory constructed by the Franco regime negated alternative accounts of the past, with memory deployed in this context for explicit political purposes.

While Martínez Sierra does not reflect at length on the memory process through which her life-writing is formed, she does articulate in *Gregorio y yo* a vision of memory as a storehouse of the past that is accessible to the remembering subject. Noting that memory stores the past "en arquilla de madera preciosa" [in a coffer of beautiful wood] (2000, 53), which can be opened and savored, Martínez Sierra later depicts it in the following terms: "[L]a memoria es arca sellada y mágica: una vez entreabierta, deja escapar recuerdos inagotables" [Memory is a sealed and magic chest: once half-opened it allows the escape of inexhaustible recollections] (2000, 393). In a sense, Martínez Sierra's presentation of memory as a storehouse of one's past evokes the archaeological model of memory. This notion that the past exists, uncontaminated by time and experience, and is accessible to the remembering subject has been widely discarded by contemporary critics, as was discussed in chapter 1. It is significant, however, that in her cited portrayal of memory, Martínez Sierra also suggests that once the "storage chest" is opened and the past is accessed, the memory process cannot be controlled by the remembering subject.

Moreover, in her life-writing Martínez Sierra simultaneously signals an awareness of the selective nature of memory, noting that she elects only to remember positive aspects, the "horas serenas" [serene hours], of her past: "Sólo las horas de serenidad he sabido guardar en la memoria" [I have only known how to keep the hours of serenity in my memory] (2000, 51). As such, she refutes any notion that the past is recovered complete and intact in her life-writing. Martínez Sierra also describes memory as "el otro nombre de nuestro 'yo'" [the other name of our "I"] (2000, 53), thus positing memory and personal identity as indistinguishable from one another. Marcus takes this notion a step further, affirming that, for some writers, "[w]ritten memory creates identity" (1994, 19), suggesting that it is the very process of life-writing that constructs the identity of the remembering self.

Of significance regarding the process of life-writing is Martínez Sierra's denial that her works constitute autobiographies. For example, she describes *Gregorio y yo* as a text "sin continuidad rigurosa ni pretensión autobiográfica" [without rigorous continuity or autobiographical pretension] (2000, 49), explicitly stating that she did not intend to produce in *Gregorio y yo* a personal, individual account: "[E]n el presente libro he llevado el propósito de huir de cuanto sea meramente personal" [In this book it has been my intention to flee from all that is merely personal] (2000, 354). However, in comparison with *Una mujer, Gregorio y yo* does deal with Martínez Sierra's private life and presents the story of the individual subject to a greater extent, leading to Blanco's description of this work as "una autobiografía literaria que narra su vida como escritora y en la cual no existe una tensión con el género ya que se conforma a él" [a literary autobiography that narrates her life as a writer and in which no tension exists with the genre, since it conforms to it] (1989, 37). This element notwithstanding, the fragmentary and nonchronological approach adopted by Martínez Sierra in this work, as she recounts episodes of her literary life with Gregorio, subverts the norms of autobiographical writing, which prescribe the production of chronological, linear narratives.

In addition, Martínez Sierra emphasizes that the value of the account of the past that she produces in *Gregorio y yo* lies in the way in which her life story is intertwined with the stories of other significant figures in the cultural world. It is, then, not her own individual life story that is of interest but, rather, the fact that "esta vida mía anda mezclada con otras de los que han hecho más o menos ruido en el mundo . . . de la inteligencia española desde 1898 a 1947" [this life of mine is intertwined with others, of those who have made more or less impact on the world . . . of the Spanish intelligentsia from 1898 to 1947] (2000, 49). Martínez Sierra's affirmation in this regard brings to mind Ortega y Gasset's famous dictum "Yo soy yo y mi circunstancia" [I am myself plus my circumstance] (1963, 18), which similarly points to an individual's environment as central to the formation of his or her identity. This focus in *Gregorio y yo* on the lives of others aligns this text with traditional descriptions of the memoir, a form of writing that has been differentiated from autobiography "proper" by some critics. While Roy Pascal, for example, notes the difficulties inherent in distinguishing between these two forms, he nevertheless argues that "[i]n the autobiography proper, attention is focused on the self, in the memoir or reminiscence on others" (1960, 5).

However, as part of the ongoing debate surrounding the parameters of autobiography, contemporary critics have questioned the basis on which the generic distinction between the autobiography and the memoir is established. Marcus Billson and Sidonie Smith, for example, have argued that "[c]ritics who describe the differences in the forms in this way fail to realize that the memorialist's vision of the outer world is as much a projection and refraction of the self as the autobiographer's. The manifest content of the memoir may be different, but the latent content is likewise self-revelation" (1980, 163). Although Martínez Sierra does not consider *Gregorio y yo* to be an autobiography as such and her account may conform to what some critics term a "memoir," the text nevertheless reveals much about the author herself as autobiographical subject.

Martínez Sierra is particularly emphatic that her writing does not constitute an autobiography with regard to *Una mujer*, a text which Concha Alborg has designated the author's "pseudo-autobiography" (1996, 485) due to its nonconformity to generic conventions. In this work, Martínez Sierra explicitly states that her account is incompatible with the genre of autobiography: "No hay . . . autobiografía en estas páginas. Son, precisamente, todo lo contrario de una autobiografía, puesto que en ellas, lo mismo que en los años que las inspiraron, paso de ser protagonista de mi propio vivir a espectadora del vivir ajeno" [There is no . . . autobiography in these pages. They are exactly all that is contrary to an autobiography, given that in them, as in the years that inspired them, I pass from being the protagonist of my own lived experience to being a spectator of the lives of others] (1989, 254). As with *Gregorio y yo,* it is the fact that this work focuses on the lives and experiences of others, rather than on the individual life story of the remembering subject, that distances it from autobiography, according to Martínez Sierra. In this way, the author shows an awareness of the fact that traditional autobiographical writing privileges the individual, public persona.

While in *Una mujer* Martínez Sierra recounts episodes of her experience as a political figure during the years of the Second Republic and Civil War, the focus of her work is not placed on her individual historical role nor on her public achievements in her career. Rather, this text has a distinctly political focus, highlighting her role as a participant in a wider struggle for social change and seeking to demonstrate the worth of the cause that she espoused. Such an emphasis is characteristic of the life-writing produced by female political figures, as Martha Watson has argued in her study of the autobiographies of women activists: "They do not claim individual distinction; rather it is their devotion to and activities for causes that make their lives worthy of recording" (1999, 104). That this is to be the focus of *Una mujer* is apparent from the very start of the text. Martínez Sierra's account opens, not with information regarding the author's life and early years, as does a conventional autobiography, but rather with an explanation of the way in which her political consciousness was formed. This opening to Martínez Sierra's work emphasizes that it is the birth and development of her political persona that is of significance in the text, rather than elements of her personal life. As such, Martínez Sierra's account may be considered to constitute a continuation of her propagandizing work for the socialist cause.

In this respect, Martínez Sierra's motivation for producing this text is quite different to that of the other women included in this study, particularly Baroja and Méndez. Martínez Sierra appears to be less concerned in *Una mujer* with the project of constructing the self through life-writing and inserting herself into the literary and historical record of her country, elements which are pertinent, to different degrees, to both Baroja and Méndez. Rather, Martínez Sierra seeks to document a political past as a means of publicizing both the work carried out by the Socialists during the period in question and also the injustices of the society that they were striving to transform.[11] *Una mujer* thus becomes, in a sense, an extension of Martínez Sierra's public advocacy.

The collective, rather than individual, focus of the account that Martínez Sierra produces in *Una mujer* serves to distance her work further from traditional notions of an autobiography. Moreover, this aspect of her work underlines its political intent, evoking notions of collective action and community spirit relevant to the socialist ideology to which Martínez Sierra subscribed. Such a move away from a focus on the individual subject to a highlighting of collective political action to effect change is reflected in the title of this work, *Una mujer por caminos de España*. This title does not privilege Martínez Sierra's important political roles nor her visibility at the time as an orator; rather, it simply positions her as a woman who traveled the roads of her country in defense of a political cause.

As well as rejecting the idea that *Una mujer* is an autobiography, Martínez Sierra likewise differentiates her account from history, conceding that, despite her active involvement in the political sphere, "[y]o ignoro demasiado para poder historiar" [I am too uninformed to be able to write a history] (1989, 217). She thus acknowledges that her life-writing can provide only a partial and incomplete record of the historical past. The lack of objectivity on the part of the author, an inevitable element in the process of life-writing, is linked by Martínez Sierra directly to her political role. Accepting that even party representatives do not necessarily have access to the full truth regarding political events, Martínez Sierra acknowledges the blind faith that one must hold in the party (1989, 217). That Martínez Sierra's intention is not to produce strictly factual historical accounts in her life-writing is also apparent in *Gregorio y yo*, in which dates and other details included by the author are often inaccurate. Such inaccuracies serve to highlight the fact that this is memory writing, rather than a fully documented history and, as such, it is susceptible to the distortions and omissions that characterize reconstructions of the past based on memory.

It is, then, Martínez Sierra's selected memories of her experiences as a female political figure in the 1930s that she recounts in *Una mujer*. Her work reveals the challenges that she faced in this role, due to both the prevailing prejudices against women in positions of power and also the masculinist nature of the political world itself, as she expresses an awareness of the anomalous nature of her role as a female political representative and as a public speaker. Recalling a political meeting in a village in southern Spain, Martínez Sierra describes her appearance as orator as an "[a]contecimiento hasta aquel día desconocido" [event unknown before that day] (1989, 139), going on to make the following observation regarding her singularity in this sociohistorical context: "Hay que darse cuenta de lo que podía hace dieciséis años significar en aquel rincón de Andalucía mora, el hecho de que una mujer se lanzase a una actividad pública y política" [It is important to realize what it meant, sixteen years ago in that corner of Moorish Andalusia, for a woman to embark on public and political activity] (1989, 139). Public speaking thus places Martínez Sierra in yet another arena considered taboo for women; moreover, she directs many of her political speeches to women, who are not the traditional audience for such discourse (1989, 89, 140). That the act of public speaking is deemed to be inappropriate for women is confirmed by critic Karlyn Kohrs Campbell, who affirms that "rhetorical action of any sort was, as defined by gender roles, a masculine activity" (1989, 10). Martínez Sierra herself notes the greater weight given to speeches made by her male colleagues, commenting that "siempre parece tener más autoridad la palabra de un hombre que la de una mujer" [a man's word always seems to have greater authority than that of a woman] (1989, 228–29).

It is perhaps in part due to this prejudice that Martínez Sierra was initially reluctant to speak in public on behalf of her party. However, the primary reason for her hesitation was, she affirms, her lack of knowledge about political theory and socialist doctrine. Recalling that it was the issues of poverty and injustice in Spanish society that initially led to her decision to join the Socialist Party, Martínez Sierra writes that "su doctrina y su filosofía no han influido gran cosa en mi decisión, y . . . cuando empecé a 'militar en sus filas,' filosofía y doctrina me eran desconocidas casi en absoluto. Y éste era mi temor al empezar mi después intensa carrera de propagandista" [their doctrine and philosophy did not have a great influence on my decision, and . . . when I began to "serve in their ranks" I knew almost nothing about philosophy and doctrine. And this was my fear when I embarked on my intense career as a propagandist] (1989, 82).

The author's misgivings about accepting a public speaking role evoke similar sentiments expressed in the life-writing of Dolores Ibárruri who, like Martínez Sierra, chose to direct many of her addresses to the women of Spain. Martínez Sierra recalls in *Una mujer* an occasion on which she and Ibárruri participated together in a political rally prior to the 1936 elections, along with socialist orator Matilde de la Torre. In her description of this event, Martínez Sierra focuses on the common purpose that the women shared despite their different party affiliations: "Aquella tarde, tres mujeres, por encima de toda doctrina, estábamos unidas en una sola voluntad. Queríamos que las izquierdas ganasen las elecciones" [That afternoon we three women, over and above any doctrine, were united in a single will. We wanted the left to win the elections] (1989, 223). This emphasis on the spirit of cooperation that existed between these female political figures is significant, given the marked lack of such collaboration between the political groups that these women represent during the period in question.[12]

Further parallels may be drawn between Martínez Sierra's *Una mujer* and Ibárruri's *El único camino* [They Shall Not Pass] (1992). Both these female political figures produce politically motivated accounts which detail their own activity on behalf of their respective parties prior to and during the Spanish Civil War, while simultaneously defending the roles played in the historical events of this period by the organizations they represent. More specifically, Martínez Sierra's descriptions of the poverty and ignorance that she encountered during her visits to villages in rural Spain resemble Ibárruri's portrayals of the dismal existence of the working classes during these years, with both writers attributing this situation to the oppressive class system in place in their country.[13] Although there are, then, certain points of comparison between both the experiences and the life-writing of Martínez Sierra and the Communist leader, Ibárruri undoubtedly achieved far greater prominence than did Martínez Sierra, becoming an international symbol for the Republican war effort. Moreover, Ibárruri continued her political career in the postwar period, holding the positions of secretary general and then president of the Spanish Communist Party during her years of exile. In contrast, Martínez Sierra withdrew from political life before the end of the Civil War.

The issue of social class, the question that initially drew both Martínez Sierra and Ibárruri to politics, is particularly relevant with regard to Martínez Sierra's life-writing. While, like the other three women included in this study, Martínez Sierra came from a comfortable, middle-class background, unlike Baroja and Méndez she was also in close contact with poor and working-class sectors of the population as part of her political work, as was León, although to a lesser extent. Martínez Sierra was thus more distanced from the idealistic, art-for-art's-sake elements of the literary world of the 1920s, and may be associated with the more socially committed tendencies of the period. In the 1930s, Martínez Sierra took the political commitment demonstrated by many writers and artists of the day a step further than most of her contemporaries through her activism and formal political responsibilities. She expresses an identification with the struggles of the poor and underprivileged groups in her country, as she recounts her encounters with the terrible reality of their lives during her visits to rural Spain in the early 1930s. Referring to these rural communities, Martínez Sierra specifies the need to communicate with and educate this sector of the population regarding alternative social models, affirming that "ésta es la masa que hay que despertar a la idea de que el hombre no es necesariamente enemigo del hombre, de que sólo con la ayuda mutua puede salvarse y lograr su destino. Esta fue la más emocionante tarea de nuestra propaganda en los primeros años de nuestra segunda república" [these are the masses that we must wake up to the idea that man is not necessarily the enemy of man, that only with mutual help can they save themselves and achieve their destiny. This was the most exciting task of our propaganda in the first years of our Second Republic] (1989, 99).

For Martínez Sierra, then, these are the people whom socialism must save, through education, higher wages, and improved social services. This thus became the focus of her political action, leading her to criticize the formal political sphere of which she was also a part, and in which, she affirms, "medio de millares de representantes del pueblo pasan horas y días en disputas políticas" [large numbers of representatives of the people spend hours and days in political disputes] (1989, 177–78). Martínez Sierra thus became disillusioned with the dominant political structures in place in her country, suggesting that these were ineffectual in achieving change for the lower classes in Spain. This rejection of the parliamentary system on Martínez Sierra's part is evidenced by the fact that in *Una mujer* she makes no specific reference to her role in the *Cortes,* despite the fact that she was an active participant in parliamentary debates during her term as a member of Parliament.

It was particularly the women in the poor rural communities of Spain whom Martínez Sierra sought to educate and inspire. However, in *Una mujer* she recalls the obstacles that she encountered in her efforts to make contact with the women in the villages that she visited. Primary among these was the conservative ideology that prevailed in such villages, perpetuating the state of ignorance and resignation in which many women lived. Martínez Sierra recounts the difficulties of making women aware of the need for education and of the importance of achieving the right to vote. For example, when Martínez Sierra attempted to raise with women of one particular village the financial problems brought by women having between ten

and twenty children each, as well as associated issues of the need for
all children to receive a certain level of education, the responses she
received were that "[l]os críos los manda Dios" [children are sent
by God] (1989, 180) and "[e]so de leer es cosa de hombres" [that
reading is men's business] (1989, 181). On a more fundamental
level, Martínez Sierra recalls the difficulties in actually finding
women to talk to in Granada, noting that their exclusion from public spaces renders them invisible in the public sphere: "[L]as mujeres no están, las mujeres no existen ni en la Casa del Pueblo, ni en
las calles, ni en los cafés" [There are no women; women do not
exist, neither in the *Casa del Pueblo,* nor in the streets, nor in the
cafes] (1989, 129).[14] Martínez Sierra thus acknowledges here the
gendering of the public/private spatial division, the dichotomy that
is at the center of feminist criticisms of patriarchy. This separation
of spheres that dictates the spaces that are open to men and women
is analyzed by Griselda Pollock in her study of the work of women
artists in relation to notions of modernity and femininity. With reference to female artists of the late nineteenth century, Pollock affirms
that "[a] range of places and subjects was closed to them while open
to their male colleagues who could move freely with men and
women in the socially fluid public world of the streets, popular entertainment and commercial or casual sexual exchange" (1988, 62).
Such a compartmentalization of space similarly operates in the context pertinent to Martínez Sierra, particularly in urban environ-
ments.[15]

One specific element of Martínez Sierra's feminist vision that she
articulates in *Una mujer* relates to the question of women's suffrage.
The controversial decision made by the Republic in 1931 to grant
equal voting rights to men and women over the age of twenty-three
is discussed in some detail by Martínez Sierra in this text. Describing
the policy as a risk taken by the government, she also notes that
Spanish women had not generally considered this issue to be a prior-
ity, affirming that being able to vote "en realidad le ha interesado
poco [a la mujer española]" [has in reality been of little interest (to
Spanish women)] (1989, 123). In this way, Martínez Sierra reveals
her understanding of Spanish political culture of this period and of
the emerging feminist movement in Spain, neither of which tended
to focus on political rights. For the women's organizations of early
twentieth-century Spain, improving women's civil and social rights
was considered to be the primary goal. Martínez Sierra herself was,
however, in favor of female suffrage in principle, despite her aware-

ness that such legislation might jeopardize the parliamentary majority held by the Left.

Martínez Sierra's support for this development was in line with the policy of her political organization, as the Spanish Socialist Party was the only political party to officially support granting women the vote in 1931. Based on the ideology that both male and female workers were oppressed under the class system and that the working class as a group was to be the revolutionary force that would bring about social change, female suffrage was considered a necessary step toward the achievement of sexual equality.[16] There was, nevertheless, ambivalence, if not overt opposition, both within the Socialist Party and among other political groups to women's suffrage, largely due to the assumption that women would vote conservatively, influenced by the Catholic church. When there was a dramatic swing from the left to the right in the first national elections in which women were able to vote, there was widespread agreement that female voters had been largely responsible for this shift. This is a view that has been expressed by many historians; well-known scholar Hugh Thomas, for example, affirms in his study of the Spanish Civil War and its origins that "the introduction of votes for women, for the first time in Spain, profited the Right" (1989, 103), although he does also make reference to other factors that influenced the result.[17]

In her own reflections in *Una mujer* on the causes of the Republican defeat in the elections of November 1933, Martínez Sierra echoes the popular interpretation that the female vote was largely responsible for the result. The author attributes this both to women's lack of preparedness for political responsibility and also to the anti-Republican campaign launched by the clergy and other conservative groups: "[S]upongo que ellas, manejadas por fuerzas más ocultas, flexibles y astutas que las nuestras, nos hicieron perder las elecciones" [I presume that they, manipulated by forces more concealed, flexible, and cunning than ours, caused us to lose the elections] (1989, 127). Martínez Sierra's explanation of the election result, then, does not place the blame on the female voters themselves. Rather, her comments are a strong indictment of the church's control of women, evidenced by the following affirmation: "No es que la mujer española sea demasiado católica. Su clero la ha dejado durante tantos siglos en tal ignorancia que, a decir verdad, pocas son las españolas que saben lo que dicen al recitar . . . el Credo" [It is not that Spanish women are excessively Catholic. Their priests have left them in such ignorance over so many centuries that, to tell the truth, there are few Spanish women who know what they are saying when they recite . . . the Creed] (1989, 125). It is this overwhelmingly conservative influence, affirms Martínez Sierra, that made many Republicans fear the consequences of female suffrage.

However, later in the text, Martínez Sierra attributes the 1933 election result to other factors, thus apparently shifting her position and downplaying the influence of female voters: "[E]n las elecciones de 1933, gracias al absurdo sistema electoral y a nuestra torpeza fundada en un poco de engreimiento, sacaron mayoría las derechas, aun cuando las izquierdas tuviéramos más votos" [In the 1933 elections, thanks to the absurd electoral system and our stupidity based on a degree of vanity, the right gained the majority, even though the left had more votes] (1989, 141). Likewise, some recent studies have suggested that the swing to the right in the 1933 elections was not necessarily due to women's conservative votes, arguing that the situation was, in fact, more complex than traditional interpretations indicate. Based on his analysis of election data, Gerard Alexander, for example, contends that the "results are better explained by a model that assumes that voters of both genders were responding to substantive events and issues" (1999, 353). Martínez Sierra's position regarding this question appears inconclusive, although her account seems to suggest that a number of factors contributed to the defeat of the left in 1933, not only the female vote.

Although much of Martínez Sierra's political action focused on women of the lower classes, she was simultaneously engaged in activities directed at women of the middle classes, through her essays and her participation in the different feminist organizations of the period.[18] She noted, in fact, that significant efforts needed to be made in order to raise the levels of awareness of social issues among middle-class women. Referring to the Asociación de Educación Cívica, Martínez Sierra affirmed in a 1933 interview that this organization "tiene por objeto principal despertar a las mujeres de la clase media, mucho más dormidas e ignorantes que las del pueblo, a la conciencia de una responsabilidad ciudadana" [has as its main objective to awaken middle-class women, who are less aware and more ignorant than working-class women, to the consciousness of having a civic responsibility] (quoted in Rodrigo 1994, 240). While the various women's groups of this period certainly played important roles in terms of creating fora in which women could gather to discuss cultural and political issues and express their concerns, Martínez Sierra indicates in *Una mujer* an awareness of the limitations of such organizations in the context in which they operated and of the limited number of women who had access to such networks: "Nuestras campañas sin duda han llegado a unos cuantos grupos selectos de la clase media madrileña, pero los entusiasmos de las afiliadas a Liceum-Club y a la Asociación Femenina de Educación Cívica, hogares de nuestro feminismo, en gran parte no son . . . sino una especie de snobismo de buen tono" [There is no doubt that our campaigns have reached certain select groups of the Madrid middle class, but the enthusiasm of the members of the Lyceum Club and the Feminine Association for Civic Education, homes of our feminism, are largely nothing more . . . than a form of fashionable snobbishness] (1989, 123–24). Martínez Sierra thus signals an understanding of the generally ineffectual nature of the feminist movement in Spain during this period and points to the complex interaction of questions of class and gender.

Martínez Sierra's assessment of the Lyceum Club distances her from her contemporaries, many of whom considered the Lyceum to be at the forefront of efforts to improve women's social situation and who praised the organization as an important site for women's intellectual advancement. However, Martínez Sierra's political knowledge and experience gave her a greater understanding of the limits of such organizations, which were firmly positioned within middle-class bourgeois society and were distanced from the very real daily struggles of many Spanish women. Her view that the Lyceum Club catered only to a minority of women is confirmed by Scanlon, who affirms that "its principal function consisted in providing a meeting place and cultural centre for a small group of educated women; its sphere of influence was relatively small" (1986, 212). Martínez Sierra's involvement with the Lyceum Club ended in 1930, presumably due to her increasing political responsibilities, although the Club itself did not close until the end of the Civil War in 1939.

Unlike many of her contemporaries, Martínez Sierra was not forced to flee Spain at the time of the Republican defeat, as she had already taken up residence in France in 1938. However, the political situation in Spain obviously precluded her from returning to her homeland. The author's experiences as exiled subject are not the focus of either *Una mujer* or *Gregorio y yo*, although Martínez Sierra did complete the latter text from exile in Argentina and makes reference at the end of her account to the fact that she is now writing from "la otra orilla" [the other shore] (2000, 365) of Latin America.

As noted previously, both of Martínez Sierra's autobiographical texts were first published in the early 1950s; that is, in the first years of her exile in the Americas, thus excluding the representation of her later experiences. While, strictly speaking, Martínez Sierra was in exile in France from 1938 to 1950, she had spent a lot of time in southern France since the 1920s, so it was, in a sense, a second home for her. It was, moreover, still within the familiar environment of Europe. That Martínez Sierra was unlikely to have experienced the overwhelming sense of loss resulting from the social and cultural displacement produced by the war from which many of her compatriots suffered is confirmed by Blanco, who affirms that "[l]a realidad del exilio sólo se le hará patente al establecerse en la capital argentina" [the reality of exile would only become patently obvious to her when she established herself in the Argentine capital] (2000, 41). However, in addition to the geographical exile caused by the Civil War, O'Connor argues that Martínez Sierra experienced various forms of metaphorical exile during her adult life: "The internal and professional exile of hidden authorship by writing under Gregorio's name, a self-exile in France, when Gregorio was living in Madrid with Catalina Bárcena, and a third exile, after Gregorio's death . . . when she felt 'exiled' from her literary identity ('Gregorio Martínez Sierra') and had to sign her works with an unfamiliar name: her own" (2000, 277). In addition, O'Connor makes reference to the difficulties that Martínez Sierra encountered after Gregorio's death in having her works published or staged, due to her lack of identity in the literary world (2000, 284).

It is the complex opposition between identity and anonymity that is central to the study of María Martínez Sierra's life-writing. Her two autobiographical texts, *Una mujer por caminos de España* and *Gregorio y yo,* demonstrate the stark contrast between this writer's public role at the center of the political world and her chosen position on the periphery of the literary arena. The former text's presentation of Martínez Sierra as feminist activist and Socialist campaigner is largely a political treatise, based both on the doctrinal principles of the Socialist movement to which Martínez Sierra subscribed and on the author's firsthand knowledge and experience, gained during her political travels through Spain in the 1930s. *Gregorio y yo,* Martínez Sierra's account of her "collaborative" literary career with her husband, reveals her negotiation of her difficult position as a female writer in the masculinist cultural sphere. Throughout her account, Martínez Sierra downplays the gender differences that existed in the literary community in which she participated, representing her seamless integration into a male-dominated literary world. However, Martínez Sierra simultaneously highlights the exclusionary nature of that environment, evidenced by her masking of her own literary identity. Martínez Sierra's memory writing thus reveals the complexities inherent in the construction of a female identity within the literary, cultural, and political establishments of early twentieth-century Spain.

4

María Teresa León (1903–1988), *Memoria de la melancolía:* The Politics of Memory

Mᴀʀíᴀ ᴛᴇʀᴇsᴀ ʟᴇóɴ, ᴡʜᴏsᴇ *ᴍᴇᴍᴏʀɪᴀ ᴅᴇ ʟᴀ ᴍᴇʟᴀɴᴄᴏʟíᴀ* ɪs ᴛʜᴇ sᴜʙ-ject of my discussion in this chapter, is the most widely known of the writers included in this study. Her visibility, however, has tended to be due primarily to her political and cultural activities and her relationship with Rafael Alberti, rather than to her literary accomplishments. The question of the construction and inscription of memory, both personal and historical, is central to León's autobiography, a text first published in Argentina in 1970, some seven years before León's eventual return to Spain after thirty-eight years of exile. In this section of my study, I seek to explore the ways in which León's *Memoria de la melancolía* opens up for debate the complex dynamics of the politics of memory and the limits of remembering, and this writer's presentation of the role of the female intellectual during the years of the Second Republic and the Spanish Civil War.

Written in the 1960s, and thus the result of many years of reflection, *Memoria* presents fragments of León's life story from the time of her childhood and adolescence through to her situation as exile in Italy at the time of writing. Born in Logroño in La Rioja, León spent most of her early years in Burgos, although her family also lived in Madrid and Barcelona for short periods. In her work, León describes the conservative nature of her upbringing in an economically privileged social milieu and the limited education that she received at the various Catholic schools that she attended. She was, in fact, expelled from one of these due to her lack of conformity, as she recalls in *Memoria,* writing in the third person: "Pocos meses antes, María Teresa León había sido expulsada suavemente del Colegio del Sagrado Corazón . . . porque se empeñaba en hacer el bachillerato, porque lloraba a destiempo, porque leía libros prohibidos" [A few months before, María Teresa León had been gently expelled from the College of the Sacred Heart . . . because she was deter-mined to do the baccalaureate, because she cried at inopportune moments, because she read prohibited books] (1998, 142).[1] Read-ing and study were thus clearly perceived to be negative influences on girls and women, further evidenced by the fact that León was told that "[p]or ahí entra el diablo" [through there the devil enters] (1998, 141). The author summarizes her family and educational en-vironment by describing it as being ruled by the "menacing" word "decency" (1998, 113), with a strict social code designed to govern her conduct: an upbringing that reflects the reality of life for the majority of young women of the middle and upper classes during this period.

However, while León notes her disconformity with the bourgeois values of her family and her traditional education, and she is unde-niably critical of these aspects of her past, she does not make refer-ence in *Memoria* to a definitive split with her family, nor does she indicate that her relatives impeded her participation in literary and cultural endeavors in the 1920s and 1930s. León does reflect on her relationship with her mother, recalling the way in which they be-came distanced from one another due to her mother's disapproval of her daughter's decisions and actions: "[M]e alejé de ti porque . . . absolutamente todo lo que hacía . . . lo encontrabas fuera de propós-ito, desprovisto de sentido . . . Sentí que me considerabas tu fracaso" [I distanced myself from you because . . . absolutely everything that I did . . . you found out of place, devoid of sense . . . I felt that you considered me to be your failure] (1998, 219). León does neverthe-less maintain some contact with her family, and returns to the family home following the breakup of her first marriage. In terms of family support, then, León was relatively privileged, especially if her situa-tion is compared to that of Baroja and Méndez.[2]

Moreover, the young León was simultaneously exposed to liberal ideals in her extended family environment, and thus had access to alternative, nontraditional models. Of particular significance was the influence of her aunt, María Goyri, one of the first Spanish women to attend university, and her uncle, the well-known scholar Ramón Menéndez Pidal.[3] In their home and in that of another of her uncles, León was free to read the previously mentioned forbid-den books and was introduced to a world in which literature and culture were highly valued and were not considered to be exclusively male domains. As a young woman, León was, moreover, aware of the stark contrast between her own life and that of her cousin Jimena, who received a liberal education at the Institución Libre de Enseñ-anza [Institute of Independent Education], did not attend mass and was allowed to go out without a chaperone (León 1998, 150–52). León articulates the importance of such alternative models on her own formation in her autobiography: "[F]ui siguiendo los pasos de Jimena y cierto aprendizaje para mi vida" [I went following in Jimena's footsteps, a sort of apprenticeship for my own life] (1998, 151).

León's adolescent years are marked also by her early marriage in 1918 to Gonzalo de Sebastián, an unhappy relationship which ended a decade later when she left her husband, despite family and social pressure to remain married. León's decision to separate from her husband resulted in her losing custody of her two sons, born in 1921 and 1925. It is significant that both her first husband and her children from this relationship are nameless in León's *Memoria*, pointing to the unhappy nature of the author's memories of this period and the lack of identification that she feels with her past self as young wife and mother.

It was also during the 1920s that León initiated her literary career, writing for the *Diario de Burgos* newspaper under the pseudonym of Isabel Inghirami, and publishing her first volume of short stories in 1928. From this time on, León's literary production was both prolific and diverse, encompassing short stories, novels, novelized biograph-ies, plays, film scripts, and a travel book, as well as political publica-tions.[4] Her accomplishments as a writer have, however, tended to be overshadowed both by her husband's fame and by her own political and cultural activism in the 1930s. León moved to Madrid in 1929 to advance her studies, and it was in the capital that she came to participate fully in the cultural scene of the day, meeting many art-ists and writers and joining the Lyceum Club. In 1930 León met Al-berti, who was to be her lifelong companion in a relationship that she portrays as a rich creative partnership. With the advent of the Second Republic, the couple were able to formalize their union, after León sought a divorce from her former husband.

During this period in Madrid, León also became actively involved in the political sphere, recording in her autobiography her partici-pation, together with Alberti, in the activities of the Spanish Com-munist Party (PCE) and, later, in the Republican war effort. In 1932, León and Alberti were granted a fellowship to study European the-atre, and they embarked on a study tour that included visits to a number of European countries, including the USSR, a trip that gave the couple new insights into politically engaged theater. They returned to Moscow in 1934 to attend a Writers' Congress, and then went on to spend over a year away from Spain due to the revolution in Asturias in October 1934 and the ensuing Republican government repression of left-wing activists. During this period abroad, León and Alberti spent time in Paris and other European cities, before traveling to the United States to give lectures on the political situation in Spain, at the urging of Communist leader Palmiro Togliatti. They then spent much of 1935 in Mexico, also visiting a number of Central American countries, before returning to Spain in time to campaign for the Popular Front elections to be held in February 1936.

During the years of the Civil War, León was at the forefront of a number of the cultural activities organized in the Republican zone. She was involved in the establishment of the Alianza de Intelectuales Antifascistas [Alliance of Antifascist Intellectuals], serving as the organization's first secretary, and set up the short-lived Teatro de Arte y Propaganda [Theater of Art and Propaganda] in 1937, followed by the more successful Guerrillas del Teatro [Guerrilla Theater], a group that traveled to the frontlines to take theatrical productions to the Republican soldiers. León both wrote and directed works for this theater company, as well as taking on acting roles on occasion. When the Republican government was forced to move to Valencia in 1937, León remained in Madrid and was a key member of the Junta de Defensa y Protección del Tesoro Artístico Nacional [Committee for the Defense and Protection of National Artistic Treasures]. Her account of their task to oversee the removal to safety in Valencia of a large number of precious art works housed in the Prado Museum and in the Monastery of El Escorial is a particularly moving part of her autobiography.[5]

At the end of the war, León and Alberti moved to Paris, where they worked for Radio France until the German invasion in 1940 forced the couple to flee to Argentina, where they spent the next twenty years of their lives and where their daughter, Aitana, was born in 1941. During their years of exile in Argentina, León's literary production was particularly prolific, as she published novels, short stories, biographies, film scripts, and essays, as well as giving regular radio broadcasts. In 1963, León and Alberti moved to Rome, and it was during her years of exile in Italy that León wrote *Memoria de la melancolía.*

León's long experience of exile ended in 1977, when she and Alberti returned to Spain following the legalization of the Spanish Communist Party. However, by this time León was already suffering from Alzheimer's disease and was thus not able to take pleasure in the long-awaited return to her homeland. The last years of León's life were spent in a clinic on the outskirts of Madrid, where she died in 1988.

Memoria de la melancolía is widely regarded as León's best work, with critics describing her autobiography as "her most lyrical and beautiful work" (Mangini 2001, 183) and "her most important feminist legacy" (Vosburg 2001, 273). It is also the most well-known of her literary works. Originally published in Argentina in 1970, *Memoria* first appeared in Spain in 1977, and has been the subject of a significant amount of critical attention in recent years, particularly since the author's death in 1988. In addition, the reedition of *Memoria* by Castalia in 1998, in a volume introduced by Gregorio Torres Nebrera, further served to stimulate interest in her work, as did the large number of conferences and publications that were organized in 2003 to commemorate the centenary of León's birth.[6] Despite such attention, León continues to be remembered primarily as the partner of Alberti and as a cultural activist, facets of her identity that the author herself chose to emphasize over her identity as a writer, as will be discussed in this chapter.

The focus of León's *Memoria* with regard to the memory process sets it apart from the autobiographies of this historical period produced by most of her contemporaries, and from the life-writing of the other women included in this study. This author explicitly acknowledges the construction of the self and of the past inherent in the autobiographical process, theorizing about the concept of memory in her own memory writing. Such an approach is unusual; as we have seen, many autobiographical narratives tend to present the past as if it were objectively and wholly available to the remembering subject, in an attempt to lend authority to the work and to attest to its veracity. This tendency is particularly evident in works produced in the sociopolitical context pertinent to León and to this study. Due to the ideologically polarized nature of Spanish society during the period in question, many writers adamantly defend the factuality of their accounts and refute versions of the past produced by their political rivals.[7] While León's own narrative is undeniably shaped by her political views, as will be discussed, she does not claim to provide an objective and complete account of the historical period in question.

It is, instead, the cultural wealth of pre–Civil War Spain that León seeks to emphasize in *Memoria*. Interweaving her own life story with those of many of her contemporaries, she pays tribute to a whole generation of Republican intellectuals who sought to preserve the ideals of democratic Spain during the war years and throughout their decades of exile. León and Alberti became central figures in the literary and cultural scene of late 1920s and early 1930s Madrid, becoming known not only as writers, but also as political activists and public speakers. León's talent as an orator is indicated by Marcos Ana, who affirms that "I never saw a woman, other than La Pasionaria, put so much passion and capacity for communication into her words" (1989, 42), thus noting both León's exceptionality as a female public speaker and her comparability to Dolores Ibárruri.[8] In addition, León and Alberti coedited the revolutionary journal *Octubre* in the 1930s, a publication in which many prominent writers of the day collaborated. Their circle of friends and acquaintances constitutes a veritable who's who of twentieth-century culture, both in Spain—María Goyri, Emilia Pardo Bazán, Zenobia Camprubí, Juan Ramón Jiménez, Federico García Lorca, Pablo Picasso, Miguel de Unamuno, and the list goes on—and on the international scene—Pablo Neruda, Joseph Stalin, Bertold Brecht, Ernest Hemingway, Diego Rivera, Octavio Paz, to name but a few.[9] León's descriptions in *Memoria* of her encounters with these figures provide fascinating insights into the world of contemporary art and culture. Poems and songs from the period are quoted throughout León's text, serving as a celebration of the cultural production of this generation.

In particular, León's work functions to a degree as a biography of her husband and a tribute to his creative talents, as she recounts the development and publication of his various works. That Alberti's story should be central to the self-defining efforts of León's autobiographical text reflects a characteristic of much life-writing; as Marcus notes, "[r]ecounting one's own life almost inevitably entails writing the life of an other or others" (1994, 273). León affirms in *Memoria* that many doors were opened to her due to Alberti's fame, thus pointing to the fact that her relationship with such a prominent writer gave her access to models and experiences that would not otherwise have been available to her. The couple were, for example, received by Stalin during a visit to Moscow, with León commenting that "[l]e habían dicho que Rafael era un poeta español querido por su pueblo . . . Yo, una mujer" [they had told him that Rafael was a Spanish poet beloved by his people . . . I, a woman] (1998, 179).

Such a summary of their respective roles reflects the way in which León was considered to hold a distinctly secondary position to her poet husband Alberti in both literary and political circles, a subordination replicated by the author's own reference to herself as "la cola del cometa" [the tail of the comet] (1998, 222).

It is noteworthy that in her autobiography León praises the decision made by her contemporary Zenobia Camprubí to remain in a secondary position to her partner, poet and Nobel Prize winner Juan Ramón Jiménez, admiring Camprubí's decision to "vivir al lado del fuego y ser la sombra" [live at the side of the fire and be the shadow] (1998, 516). It appears that León herself made a similar choice. She does, however, signal the important role played by women in the lives of the famous male writers of her generation, even suggesting that the Nobel Prize was won as much by Camprubí as by Jiménez. Moreover, it is important to bear in mind, when considering León's apparent acceptance of a position subordinate to her husband, the realities of her sociohistorical context, as Mangini elucidates: "If we criticize Leon's submission in the face of her subordinate condition, it is fundamental to bear in mind that monster of one head, but an omnipotent head: Spain's prevailing misogyny" (2001, 185).

Despite the misogynistic climate to which Mangini refers and that undeniably extended to the cultural arena, León does not criticize the gendered nature of the Madrid literary scene of her day in *Memoria*. In this way, her perspective is quite different from those of Baroja and Méndez, both of whom are highly critical of the exclusionary politics of the literary world. There is no indication in León's work that she felt marginalized from the male-dominated literary community nor that any sites of intellectual practice were closed to her as a woman. Rather, León portrays herself as participating together with Alberti and their contemporaries in cultural and political pursuits, as well as literary endeavors, in a representation that is in some respects reminiscent of Martínez Sierra's portrayal of her involvement in the cultural scene.

The enduring collaborative partnership that León enjoyed with Alberti is, of course, key to her integration in this male-dominated world and is an element that differentiates León's life story from those of the other women included in this study. As we have seen, neither Baroja's husband nor her literary brothers were supportive of her endeavors, while the marriages of both Martínez Sierra and Méndez ended when their husbands left them for other women. The extent to which these latter relationships were truly collaborative partnerships is also questionable. In contrast, León's depiction of the close and productive working relationship that she and Alberti shared is confirmed by their contemporaries. Santiago Ontañón, who worked with the couple in the Teatro del Arte y Propaganda during the years of the Civil War, makes the following affirmation in this regard: "The couple were very united in their political action and the one who took the lead, as regards organization, was María Teresa León. Rafael arranged the texts and the collaboration between the two of them was close and absolute" (quoted in Monleón 1977, 38).

It is her collaboration with Alberti and with other prominent male writers of the day, as well as certain characteristics of her literary works, that has led contemporary critics to consider León to have been an important member of the "Generation of 1927," despite the fact that she is not included in traditional discussions of the canonical "generation." José María Amado, for example, declares León to have been "one of the best writers of the so-called Generation of 1927" (quoted in Torres Nebrera 1996, 9); likewise, Maya Altolaguirre describes her as "one of the most singular writers of the Generation of 1927" (2003, 11). León only moved to Madrid in 1929, and was thus perhaps not as integrated in the literary circles of the Spanish capital during that decade as were some of her contemporaries. She did, however, make regular visits to Madrid prior to 1929 and was in close contact with the writers who are deemed to belong to the "generation," as Mangini confirms: "León had been following closely the activities of the members of the Generation of 1927, with whom she was in contact in her constant journeys to Madrid before 1929" (2001, 181). Moreover, from the mid-1920s to the mid-1930s, the period in which the writers of the "generation" were publishing their key works and seeing their careers flourish, León's literary production was likewise prolific. She wrote several volumes of short stories, two dramatic works, and published numerous articles in the press and in literary journals during these years.

Pointing to parallels between León's work and that of her male peers, critics such as Vosburg (2001) and Torres Nebrera (1996, 1998) maintain that her early literary production was stylistically linked to the poetics of this canonical group of writers and reflected the dominant trends and models of the period. Moreover, the shift in León's literary production from earlier surrealist influences to more realist and overtly politically committed works reflected the broader trend of the time; many of her contemporaries, both male and female, likewise moved away from the vanguard tendencies of the cultural poetics of the 1920s to produce works that more closely reflected the political climate of the 1930s. In León's case, this change also reflected her commitment to communism and her increased activism in the political sphere, aspects which influenced the ideological tenets of her works.

León herself makes no claims with regard to her place in the canonical "Generation of 1927" in *Memoria,* although her account does clearly place her at the center of the Madrid literary circle of her day. Her autobiography tends to focus, rather, on her cultural activism in broader terms and on her political activities. Little attention is paid in *Memoria* to León as writer, despite her accomplishments and prolific production in the literary sphere. While she does signal the importance of writing for her, referring to it as a "comezón diaria" [daily itch] (1998, 476), she does not reflect on the process of creation of her different works nor on her experiences when writing these. This absence in *Memoria* is noted by Melissa Stewart, who proposes reading León's autobiography together with her fictional narrative *Juego limpio* [Fair Play] (1987), a novel first published in 1959 that, she argues, "enriches the reading of María Teresa León's life story in *Memoria de la melancolía* through the creation of a 'writerly' self that rarely appears in *Memoria* and by enacting the account of the war that she only outlines in the autobiography" (1998, 235). León's earlier novel thus provides the reader with important insights into the author's life that are missing from her memoirs.[10]

Despite the fact that there was clearly a feminist dimension to many of León's activities and writings, she did not overtly identify herself as a feminist. While she was certainly not an advocate of the prevailing ideology of domesticity that restricted women to the private sphere of the home, evidenced by her criticisms of the gender politics of the bourgeois society in which she was raised and by her own defiance of culturally imposed gender boundaries, León did not directly challenge this norm in her writings. In fact, among her publications written in exile is a practical guide for housewives, entitled *Nuestro hogar de cada día* [Our Everyday Home] (1958), which offers suggestions for dealing with a wide range of problems that women may face in the home. This work recognizes the importance of the domestic sphere in women's lives and their roles as what Torres Nebrera describes as "salvaguarda[s] de la cotidianidad del hogar" [safeguards of the daily life of the home] (1998, 42), without endorsing the discourse of domesticity that confined women to the home and to the roles of wife and mother.

The situation of women within the institution of marriage is precisely one of the aspects of patriarchal society of which León is critical, evidenced by her references in *Memoria* to the way in which a married woman is considered to be the property of her husband: "Te toman de la mano, te atraen, te besan la mano, te conviertes en su propiedad, porque eres, dicen, su propiedad" [They take you by the hand, they attract you, they kiss your hand, you become their property, because you are, they say, their property] (1998, 174). However, while León did denounce the social and economic oppression of women, whether within marriage or in other spheres of society, she did not explicitly reject women's subordination to men nor did she advocate an increase in their political rights. León's positioning in this regard reflects the social orientation of Spanish feminism at this time, which, as we have seen, focused on achieving civil and educational equality for women.[11]

The brand of feminism that León espoused was, moreover, in line with the communist doctrine that she followed, which considered the cause of women's oppression to lie in issues of economics and social class, rather than in gender per se. For León, the attainment of collective freedom and an end to the class system would result in the emancipation of all oppressed groups in society, including women. The question of the class structure that prevailed in early twentieth-century Spain is thus central to León's political concerns and to her ideological positioning, as she makes explicit in *Memoria:* "[E]l problema es la división de los hombres en llamados y olvidados, se trata de terminar con una sociedad basada en la desigualdad, en las clases" [The problem is the division of men into the called and the forgotten, it is a question of doing away with a society based on inequality, on classes] (1998, 172). Despite her own privileged background, León demonstrated solidarity with the poor and the working classes from the very start of her literary career. She openly denounced injustice and expressed "lo que pensaba de la sociedad que permite la ignorancia y la desesperación que llevan al crimen" [what I thought of a society that permits the ignorance and despair that lead to crime] (1998, 160), affirming many of those marginalized by society to be victims of an unjust system. León's defense of such groups and her contact with them through her cultural and political activities violates the boundaries between social classes, divisions that are closely associated with the discourse that distinguishes "high" from "low" culture.[12] León likewise violates the high/low dichotomy, as she is clearly part of Madrid's cultural elite and thus associated with "high" culture, while simultaneously making contact with and representing the opposite end of the social and cultural spectrum.

In her references to the literary scene of 1920s and 1930s Madrid in *Memoria,* León does not discuss in detail the role of female intellectuals within the cultural community, although she does make mention of a number of her female contemporaries and the friendships that she developed with them.[13] Some other relationships and contacts are silenced: León was, for example, present at the regular *tertulias* held at the home of Méndez and Altolaguirre, but this is not referred to in her autobiography. In addition, artist Maruja Mallo, who was an important figure in cultural circles at the time and is named by Mangini as one of the two most prominent females to figure among the "Generation of 1927," together with León herself (2001, 179), is not mentioned. It seems likely that this particular omission is due to Mallo's earlier relationship with Alberti; Mangini notes that León "prohibited Alberti from mentioning Mallo and . . . Mallo came to be a taboo topic among her counterparts of the Generation of 1927" (2001, 79).

León does refer specifically in *Memoria* to the lack of a strong network of women writers and artists at the time, signaling their general isolation from one another: "Creo que se movían por Madrid sin mucha conexión, sin formar un frente de batalla" [I think that they were moving about Madrid without much connection, without forming a battle front] (1998, 514). One exception to which León refers is the establishment of the Lyceum Club. Noting the uniqueness of this organization in its provision of a meeting place for women, she describes the Club in positive terms, affirming the progressive nature of its goals in the context of late 1920s Spain: "El Lyceum Club no era una reunión de mujeres de abanico y baile. Se había propuesto adelantar el reloj de España" [The Lyceum Club was not a meeting of women who like to dance and wave their fans. It was intended to advance Spain's clock] (1998, 515). León also notes the criticisms directed at the Club and its members by conservative groups, deploying a tone of comicality in her descriptions of their outrage at "la sublevación de las faldas" [the uprising of the skirts] (1998, 514).

Despite her positive depiction of the Lyceum Club and its goals, it should be noted that León does not present the organization as having been of central importance for her in terms of either her personal or professional development. She did, of course, have access to other outlets for her creative talents and was undoubtedly more integrated in the cultural scene of the day than were many of her contemporaries, collaborating with her male peers. In addition, León's increased political commitment in the 1930s meant that she had less time to dedicate to her other interests. Moreover, as has been discussed in previous chapters, the Lyceum was not an overtly political organization, despite Baroja's affirmations to the contrary. As such, León might have felt less affinity with the Club as her dedication to communist doctrine developed in the 1930s, perhaps distancing her from the other Lyceum Club members. While she does not specifically state that this was the case with regard to her peers at the Lyceum, she does acknowledge in *Memoria* that the political stance that she and Alberti adopted distanced them from some of their friends and contemporaries: "[L]os amigos dejaron de saludarnos. Nos criticaban" [Our friends stopped greeting us. They criticized us] (1998, 172).[14]

As we have seen, the cultural figuration of the woman writer as a marginal figure in early twentieth-century Spain makes the act of writing, for León and her female counterparts, a distinctly political act. Such an association between writing and politics is made explicit by León. While she does not specifically refer to writing in feminist terms, she nevertheless portrays the cultural activity undertaken by herself and other intellectuals during the war as constituting a central part of the Republican war effort, a literary taking-up of arms that continued with the outbreak of the Second World War: "La guerra a la inteligencia . . . obligaba a los intelectuales del mundo a contestar con sus armas a la agresión" [The war on intelligence . . . obliged the intellectuals of the world to take up their own arms in response to the aggression] (1998, 109). Such a connection is further evidenced by León's initiative to establish the tellingly named Guerrillas del Teatro, the theater group with which she traveled to the front lines, and in her references to the war against fascism undertaken on a cultural level as "nuestra pequeña guerra" [our little war] (1998, 286), a part of the war effort whose absence from historical accounts is criticized by León.

Characterized by an acute sense of collective memory, *Memoria* is an account that goes beyond the personal life story of the author to communicate the historical experiences of a generation. It is the collective and historical aspects of León's work that lead Lydia Masanet to argue that *Memoria* should not be considered to constitute an "autobiography"; rather, she classifies the work as "a testimonial text, in which more is said about the Civil War than about Teresa León [*sic*] herself" (1998, 44). While Masanet goes on to acknowledge the difficulty of classifying León's account, her analysis tends to replicate traditional generic divisions and distinctions between forms of life-writing. Such divisions are undeniably challenged by León's work, which expresses both the political and the personal, the collective and the individual. The collective nature of *Memoria* is, for example, evidenced by the author's use of the first-person plural in her account of exile, a technique that indicates León's identification with the thousands of Spaniards who fled to France at the end of the war and suggests that her experiences represent, to some extent, those of many of her compatriots.

It should, however, be noted that in some ways León was clearly in a privileged position compared to many of the Spanish exiles in France in 1939, as Alberti's renown and the couple's links to the Communist Party and the Republican government meant that they received a great deal of assistance after they left Spain. Many Spaniards in France in the immediate postwar years suffered long periods in concentration camps, whereas León and Alberti were able to avoid arrest through their numerous contacts. Similarly, their successful flight to Argentina following the Nazi occupation of France places them among a select and fortunate group, for, as Mangini has noted, it was generally only "the relatively privileged" who were able to seek refuge in the Americas (1995, 154). Their good fortune in terms of being able to relocate to America is acknowledged by León herself (1998, 465), who cites the bond of a common language as a key factor in alleviating their feeling of isolation.

While such privilege may be seen to distance León from many of her contemporaries, her account makes explicit that she was not isolated from the realities of the conflict nor from the trauma of exile. Rather, the fact that she played an active role in the Republican cause, visiting the front lines and experiencing truly terrifying and dangerous situations, is emphasized in her work, as is the feeling of anguish engendered by the manner of her and Alberti's displacement from their homeland: "Con qué rudeza nos han separado de lo que más queríamos" [With what crudeness they have separated us from all that we held most dear] (1998, 462). Moreover, a sense of guilt is discernible in León's narrative of exile, a trait common in such accounts. As news reached them of the misery, violence, and repression in postwar Spain, particularly accounts of the persecution of and retribution against those who had supported the Republican cause, León affirms that "[n]os parecía que traicionábamos con nuestra suerte de respirar aún a tantos compañeros hundidos en la sombra de las cárceles" [it seemed to us that we were betraying so many companions lost in the shadow of the prisons, with our good fortune in still being able to breathe] (1998, 393).

In addition, her text includes numerous remembrances of friends and acquaintances who lost their lives during the conflict and in its aftermath. León thus articulates the burden that her fortunate position as a survivor of the war entails, evoking Cathy Caruth's distinction between the trauma of experience and the trauma of survival: "At the core of these stories . . . is thus a kind of double telling, the oscillation between a *crisis of death* and the correlative *crisis of life:* between the story of the unbearable nature of an event and the story of the unbearable nature of its survival" (1995, 7; italics in original). Through her life-writing, León seeks to make the fact of her survival more bearable by paying homage to her absent friends and to the hundreds of nameless Republican supporters and by inscribing the memories of the past that she knows she is in danger of losing. In this way, her writing evokes Francisco Caudet's descriptions of the importance of memory for the exiled subject as a means of both preserving and coming to terms with the past: "Memory or recall, by means of the word, language, becomes instrumental in permitting the process of recovery, of healing. The memory of the past and its verbalization are antidotes to abandonment and renunciation, to the acceptance of failure" (1997, 22).

It is these feelings of loss, displacement, and failure that contribute to the sense of melancholy that pervades León's memories and to which she refers in the title of her autobiography. With regard to this aspect of León's work, it is useful to draw on Freud's "Mourning and Melancholia," in which he affirms that melancholy "is in some way related to an object-loss which is withdrawn from consciousness, in contradistinction to mourning, in which there is nothing about the loss that is unconscious" (1984, 254). For Freud, melancholy is the result of one's inability to accept the loss of an object, generally a person who has died. Rather than entering into the process of mourning, a subject afflicted by melancholy internalizes the loss, refusing to accept the reality of the situation and embarking instead on a drawn-out process of grieving. That León dwells on the past in this way, expressing melancholy for the various losses that she has experienced in quite a passive and negative manner, seems at odds with her very active political role and the forward-looking character of the ideology to which she subscribes. However, while León's narrative bemoans the failure of her and her compatriots' attempts to defend the Republic during the Civil War, she simultaneously highlights the heroic and tenacious nature of those efforts.

In her representation of the war years in *Memoria,* León communicates the pervasiveness of fear, persecution, and death during that period, while, in a somewhat surprising affirmation, she simultaneously refers to those same years as "[d]ías felices . . . los mejores de nuestra vida" [happy days . . . the best of our lives] (1998, 380). The motivation for León's singular description of the arduous years of the Spanish Civil War as the happiest time of her life is, she explains, due to the unique spirit of camaraderie and sense of collective purpose which characterized life in the Republican zone. Moreover, this period brought opportunities for women to participate in a wide range of social, political, and cultural activities that had previously been closed to them, making this an exciting time for women such as León who chose to participate in the political and intellectual arena.[15]

León's depiction of the war years as a happy period is discussed in some detail by Ángel Loureiro, who refers to León's characterization of the war years as one of "manic elation," maintaining that these years constitute for the author a period of "glorious plenitude" (2000, 69), coming between the sorrow and displacement that dominate the rest of León's life, both before and after the war. For Loureiro, the "melancholy" of which León writes in her autobiography is neither solely nor primarily due to the historical experience of the war, which he posits as one among many episodes of loss endured by León. However, while arguing that León's work is characterized by a "lifelong obsession with severance, displacement, abandonment, and loss" (2000, 67), Loureiro is unable to identify the cause of such enduring melancholy, noting that "with the passing of narrated time it becomes increasingly difficult to specify what those losses are" (2000, 68). Such an apparent downplaying of the effect of the experience of the war on León's life is surprising, with the powerful influence of that event manifest in her text.

There is, however, certainly evidence in the work to support the notion that León's childhood and adolescence were also characterized by a sense of displacement. Describing herself as a "[n]iña de militar inadaptada siempre, . . . con amigas de paso" [a soldier's

child, always maladjusted, . . . with short-term friends] (1998, 73),
due to her family's constant moves, León communicates her dissatisfaction with her traditional gender-structured education and restrictive upbringing, as discussed. She thus recalls and constructs in her
autobiographical text an identity that is in large part constituted by
memories of exclusion. Her life story, marked by disconformity from
its very beginning, records a discordance with her environment that,
I contend, must be seen to contribute to the "sustained exile"
which, Loureiro argues (2000, 72), characterizes her life. As feminist
scholars maintain, gender as a cultural construction cannot be
evaded by any critical perspective; thus any analysis of León as autobiographical subject must take into consideration her gender positioning.

León's rejection of the paradigms of femininity dominant in her
society and her acts of rebellion against such models make her, precisely, a marginalized—or "exiled"—subject in a patriarchal world.
Critics have argued that women in a patriarchal society may be considered to be in a position of exile due to their subordination, an
association made explicit by Benstock, who states that "[f]or
women, the definition of patriarchy already assumes the reality of
expatriate *in patria*" (1989, 20). Exile, then, is both a political and a
genderic construct. It is, moreover, a psychic state, with its exten-
sions beyond merely geographical definitions confirmed by Angela
Ingram, who notes that it may take either a literal or metaphorical
form (1989, 6). León, as a child who rebels against the educational
precepts of her time, as a woman active in the political sphere, as a
Communist, and as a writer, defies culturally imposed definitions of
femininity and may therefore be seen as an exiled subject within patriarchal society, before experiencing the physical displacement of
her enforced political exile of the 1930s.[16]

León's existence, then, is characterized by continuous transit and
displacement. Increasingly distanced—geographically, politically,
and emotionally—from her homeland, León describes her years of
physical exile from Spain in terms of a quest for "una patria
pequeña como un patio o como una grieta en un muro muy sólido"
[a little homeland like a patio or a crevice in a very solid wall] (1998,
81). This *patria* is, for León, provisionally constituted in different periods of her life by France, Argentina, and Italy, but she is haunted
throughout these years by the memory of "nuestro paraíso perdido"
[our paradise lost] (1998, 98). Reiterating her affirmations regarding the sense of camaraderie and collective spirit among Spanish Re-

publicans, León suggests that her friends and her Communist political convictions constitute her *patria* in exile.

The ideological positioning of León's text is central to Loureiro's reading of *Memoria,* as he makes reference to the author's "ideological hedging" (2000, 72), her "ideological omissions and simplifications, avoidances, and distortions" (2000, 73), and her "self-interested ideological beliefs" (2000, 77). It is certainly the case, as Loureiro correctly notes, that León omits from her account references to a number of apparently pertinent historical details—the problematic issues associated with the figure of Stalin, for example, and the well-documented divisions among the forces of Republican Spain. However, rather than perceiving these omissions as evasions, I contend that they reflect the complex and shifting relationship between the past and present selves of the autobiographical narrative and the process of selection inherent in life-writing. León chooses to foreground certain aspects of the personal and historical past, silencing others, as part of her project of inscribing a history that runs contrary to official versions of the period.

Writing some thirty years after the events in question and from the standpoint of the intellectual in exile, León signals from the outset her awareness of the imprecise nature of life-writing as she enters what she describes as the "jardín cerrado" [enclosed garden] of her memories (1998, 69). On the one hand, she foregrounds her role as witness to the events that she is to describe in her account: "[D]ejo únicamente mi participación en los hechos, lo que vi, lo que sentí, lo que oí" [I leave here only my participation in the events, what I saw, what I felt, what I heard] (1998, 69). On the other hand, she simultaneously acknowledges that her recording of those events is inevitably "pasado por una confusión de recuerdos" [passed through a confusion of memories] (1998, 69), discounting any attempt to reproduce perfectly the past. There are numerous references in the text to the fallibility of memory, as she acknowledges her inability, and at times her unwillingness, to remember the past with precision: "[L]o que estoy escribiendo no tiene ni deseo de perfección ni de verdad" [What I am writing has no desire for perfection nor truth] (1998, 69). León's memories of the past are thus presented in *Memoria* as simultaneously vivid and elusive, as she seeks to preserve or control them, while acknowledging the futility of such attempts.

León rejects, moreover, models of autobiographical writing that prescribe linearity and a precise regard for chronology, presenting episodes of her life story in a fragmentary and jumbled manner. In many instances she specifies neither date nor place, details that would serve to anchor the autobiographical subject in historical time. Such a disregard for chronology radically contravenes traditional generic prescriptions, as Sidonie Smith indicates: "If specifying dates in autobiographical writing is one of the technologies whereby a text constructs the historical individual—dating makes the 'man,' so to speak—then refusing to date, refusing to fill the gaps in the chronological record, interferes with conventional technologies of developmental individuality and by implication with the laws of genre" (1993, 106).

In a further subversion of conventional models of autobiographical writing that advocate the production of stable, coherent self-narratives, the narrative voice of León's text moves from first person to second to third, an element that also contributes to the fragmentary nature of *Memoria*. In her recounting of her story of exile, for example, León uses both the first-person voice, thus emphasizing the intensely personal nature of her story—"Estoy cansada de no saber dónde morirme" [I am tired of not knowing where to die] (1998, 97)—as well as the more impersonal third-person form: "Le cuesta siempre darse cuenta de que vive en la calle del destierro" [It is always hard for her to realize that she lives on exile street] (1998, 103). Such a deployment of the third-person voice serves to create a sense of distance between León as narrator and León as subject of the narrative, thus enacting the split subject of the autobiographical text, a characteristic of this form of writing that, as Felicity Nussbaum notes, "allows for the recognition that the 'I' who is writing is distinct from the 'I' who is written about" (1989, 32). León makes explicit the presence of this characteristic of life-writing in her work, affirming that she is "como separada, mirándome" [as though split, looking at myself] (1998, 83). León's awareness of the split between the two voices or identities functioning in her autobiography is unusual. The overwhelming majority of memory writers disacknowledge memory as a process, presenting the narrating "I" and the subject of the narration as identical, thus fulfilling the autobiographical "pact" advocated by Philippe Lejeune (1989). In addition, León's use of the third-person voice in parts of her account serves to highlight her lack of identification with aspects of her past life and self.

The fragmentary nature of León's account and her reflections on the workings of memory in *Memoria* point to the author's rejection of notions of the past as fixed and stable. The favoring of a particular model of memory over others has ideological resonances, an association signaled by Nicola King, who notes that the archaeological model, which presents memories of the past as a static and unchanging collection of facts to be accessed at will, "seems to be at work in nationalist movements which appeal to an idealized organic past" (2000, 5). This is precisely the case in Francoist Spain, where an officially constructed national history, based on the rigidly defined Catholic and Falangist conception of truth, was used to support the regime's political agenda. The form of memory advocated was, as Roberta Johnson notes, a tradition that "is nostalgic, and yearns for that mythical Golden Age when all was peace, unity, and harmony within the imagined national borders" (1996, 170). León's rejection of the notion that the past can be recovered intact and that her past and present selves can be unproblematically integrated thus serves to emphasize her distance from the political regime in force in her homeland. *Memoria* suggests that the autobiographical process involves a provisional and continuous reconstruction of self and past, as opposed to the recovery of an original identity and pure history.

Furthermore, León explicitly seeks to differentiate her account from those provided by traditional historiography, noting that historical accounts of the events in question abound and referring to her lack of training as a historian. León specifies that the objective of her autobiographical narrative is to give voice to elements absent from conventional historiography and to inscribe her own personal testimony, while she is still alive to do so. This latter element entails León's recognition of the passing away of living witnesses of the Civil War, reflecting an awareness of time closing in and a consciousness that memories not now recorded will be lost. A primary objective of her narrative, the product of many years of reflection, is thus to inscribe the past to ensure that this period of Spanish history is not forgotten, enacting the function of testimony as "a means of transmission to future generations" (Wieviorka 1994, 24).

The apparently conflicting motives for testifying to a traumatic past have been explored by scholars of Holocaust writing, who signal the contradictions inherent in the process of reconstructing the past through memory. While some critics insist that the imperative of such memory work is "to remember, not to forget" (Wieviorka 1994, 30), others contend, conversely, that survivors "remember *in order to forget*" (Geyer and Hansen 1994, 176; italics in original). Precisely such a dichotomous presentation of the memory process is apparent in León's writing. On the one hand, memory is shown to be an essential element in the constitution of subjectivity, with León going so far as to affirm that remembering is more important than life itself (1998, 130). Returning to one's past through memory is portrayed as being less complicated than confronting the present (1998, 83) and is shown to bring happiness, albeit fleetingly: "[E]s el regreso de la felicidad que dura un instante" [It is the return of a happiness that lasts an instant] (1998, 114). On the other hand, memory is presented as inescapable, something that, on occasions at least, the author would like to be free of, as she comments that she wishes to experience "cosas que me sacaran el pasado de la memoria" [things that will remove the past from my memory] (1998, 93). Memory is presented here as involuntary, outside of the control of the subject. These two contrasting presentations of memory continue throughout León's text to the very end, where the author affirms that she continues to live "chained" to memories of the past (1998, 542), while maintaining the hope that her ability to remember will not diminish (1998, 544). León's foregrounding of memory and her repeated concerns regarding its fallibility are particularly poignant given that she develops Alzheimer's disease in the later years of her life, a condition that affects precisely one's capacity of recall.

León likens the act of reconstructing past and self to an attempt to complete a jigsaw puzzle, in a process by which different fragments of her life are brought together by the workings of memory, in an attempt to create a whole: "[V]uelvo a reconstruirme como hacen los niños con sus juegos de piececitas de madera" [I reconstruct myself again as children do with their games with little pieces of wood] (1998, 114). Similarly, as exiled subject León affirms that "[n]os reconstruíamos con fatiga" [we reconstructed ourselves with fatigue] (1998, 464), indicating the extent to which the trauma of exile necessitates the reconstruction of the subject. However, her narrative suggests that the sense of lack of closure with regard to her past impedes the completion of this process. For León, writing her autobiography in the 1960s with Franco still in power in Spain, her story and that of her generation remains unfinished, "una historia de la que no conozco el fin" [a story whose ending I do not know] (1998, 466). The jigsaw puzzle of past and self, then, remains incomplete.

While the cited examples suggest a degree of agency on the part of the subject in efforts to construct a sense of identity, León also emphasizes the role played by others in the formation of an individual's subjectivity: "Somos el producto de lo que los otros han irradiado de sí o perdido, pero creemos que somos nosotros . . . Somos lo que nos han hecho, lentamente, al correr tantos años" [We are the product of what others have radiated from themselves, or have lost, but we believe that we are ourselves . . . We are what they have made us, slowly, over the passage of many years] (1998, 146–47). The formation of identity is thus presented as a collaborative act, signaling the reciprocal constitution of self and other. The key role of the other in the autobiographical process has been signaled by contemporary scholars, who argue that a testimony is not a monologue; rather, bearing witness to one's past is a process that includes a listener or addressee. That the presence of an interlocutor is essential to the memory process is emphasized by Shoshana Felman, who affirms that "[m]emory is conjured . . . essentially in order to *address* another, to impress upon a listener, to *appeal* to a community" (1992, 204; italics in original).

The other to whom León directs her autobiographical narrative is multiple, as the author addresses a diverse range of people in her text, from her mother to her compatriots in exile, from the unspecified reader to the youth of 1960s Spain. She urges her fellow exiles to rectify their absence from history by articulating their experiences—"desterrados de España, . . . contad lo que nunca dijeron los periódicos, decid vuestras angustias" [exiles of Spain . . . tell what the newspapers never told, speak of your anguish] (1998, 404)—and addresses other witnesses to the events she describes, in an apparently rhetorical appeal to them to attest to the validity of her record of the past: "¿Te acuerdas, Rafael?" [Do you remember, Rafael?] (1998, 306); "¿Te acuerdas, Luis [Buñuel]?" [Do you remember, Luis (Buñuel)?] (1998, 310); "¿Recuerdas, Dolores [Ibárruri]?" [Remember, Dolores (Ibárruri)?] (369). Consciously foregrounding the dialogic nature of her writing, León makes frequent injunctions to the unidentified or generic reader, addressed as *vosotros* [you], a strategy that serves to involve the reader in the autobiographical process: "Habréis de perdonarme" [You will have to excuse me] (1998, 69); "Os lo voy a contar" [I am going to tell you about it] (1998, 112). The unremitting presence of the variously constituted other in León's work reveals the author's imperative, not only to tell, but to be heard. The problem of establishing a connection with the reader is, Ugarte contends, particularly acute in literature of exile: "A writer in exile must face the loss of a former readership and compensate for it by imagining a new one . . . The exile's potential reader is as amorphous as the condition itself" (1989, 64).

The challenge of imagining and seeking to engage with a new readership is evidenced in León's work by her injunctions to the youth of Spain. She expresses concern that this group who, she maintains, must bear the responsibility for the "resurrection" of their country (1998, 108), may be unaware of the existence and the history of the Republican exiles due to their lack of voice in their homeland during the long years of the Franco regime. Arguing that a bond of identification links the exiles to their young compatriots—"Nosotros somos ellos, lo que ellos serán cuando se restablezca la verdad de la libertad" [We are them, what they will be when the truth of freedom is re-established] (1998, 98)—León emphasizes the need for the history of Spain's recent past to continue to be voiced, recounting details of the period in question to young Spaniards who visit her in exile. However, despite sharing a common political ideology—the young people are left-wing dissidents in Spain—León struggles to communicate effectively with them: "¿Por qué me faltan las palabras claves para dialogar con ellos?" [Why do I lack the key words to converse with them?] (1998, 104). León's narrative thus discloses the problematics inherent in seeking to engage with an interlocutor or a readership in the present, those who belong to a different generation and come from a country with which she is no longer familiar.[17]

León is the only writer included in this study to relocate to Spain in the 1970s following the death of Franco, and thus to experience the long-awaited restoration of democracy in her homeland. However, her failing health and memory loss meant that she was largely unaware of the significant changes that were taking place in Spanish society during this period and of what critics have described as the *desmemoria,* or lack of historical memory, that characterized the years of the so-called "transition" from dictatorship to democracy in Spain. Signaling that this historical process was based on a need to forget the past and to eliminate collective memory of the preceding forty years in order to facilitate peaceful change, Paloma Aguilar Fernández affirms that "under the emotional call for 'national reconciliation' a thick veil was drawn over the past and it was accepted that those institutional acts of violence committed throughout the dictatorship would remain unpunished" (2001, 8).[18] That the immediate post-Franco period was, indeed, characterized by such a pact of silence and a reluctance to recall the recent past is confirmed by publications that appeared in the press at the time: an editorial in the daily newspaper *El País* in 1977, for example, asserted that "democratic Spain should, from now, look forward, forget the responsibilities and the events of the Civil War, make an abstraction of the forty years of dictatorship . . . A people cannot and should not lack historical memory: but this should serve to nourish peaceful projects of coexistence for the future and not to feed rancor about the past" (*El País* 1977). In a sense, this approach adopted in post-Franco Spain is precisely what León foreshadows in *Memoria* and is the primary motivation behind her autobiographical project, as she repeatedly and emphatically calls on her contemporaries to speak of their experiences and on Spaniards more generally not to forget the past. In this way, León's work continues to be of relevance in contemporary Spain, particularly in light of the recent calls to rearticulate Spanish history and acknowledge the problematic elements of the process of transition, led by the efforts of the Asociación para la Recuperación de la Memoria Histórica [Association for the Recovery of Historical Memory].[19] This current process in Spain, like León's narrative, points to the struggle between the state's interest in forgetting the past and the need on the part of individuals or groups to remember precisely what, for the sake of the "national interest," they are urged to forget.

A complex mixture of personal memory and historical critique, María Teresa León's *Memoria de la melancolía* foregrounds the constant negotiation between remembering and forgetting that characterizes the process of life-writing. In an autobiographical project that involves the situating and interpreting of her own past in the context of other stories and lives, León attempts to negotiate and articulate the relationship between individual and collective histories. The nonchronological nature of her writing establishes a pattern of diffusion and diversity, in keeping with the diverse approaches to memory itself revealed in her text, as she acknowledges and demonstrates that an individual's memory of the past is inevitably subject to modification by the self who remembers. While much of León's work focuses on her experiences as exiled subject, as she details the lasting effects of the social and cultural displacements produced by the war, *Memoria* also offers important insights into the role of women in the literary and cultural arenas of early twentieth-century Madrid. In particular, the opportunities for women that the changing social and gender dynamics of the 1920s and 1930s presented are highlighted in León's account of this period, as she seeks to record for posterity her contribution and that of her contemporaries to the Republican war effort and the traumatic effects of the Spanish Civil War on their lives. León's *Memoria de la melancolía* stands as a unique testimony to this period of Spanish history, written by one of the most gifted and acclaimed women writers of her generation who has long been relegated to the margins of literary history.

5

Concha Méndez (1898–1986), *Memorias habladas, Memorias armadas*: The Female Intellectual and the "Generation of 1927"

THE FOCUS OF THIS FINAL CHAPTER IS THE MEMOIRS OF CONCHA MÉNDEZ, entitled *Memorias habladas, memorias armadas,* a text that Méndez produced in collaboration with her granddaughter, Paloma Ulacia Altolaguirre, in the 1980s, and that offers important insights into the cultural and social reality of 1920s and 1930s Madrid for the female writer and intellectual. Portraying the vitality of the Madrid cultural scene during this era of significant social and political change, Méndez's text simultaneously reveals the complex interactions between women and modernity, and her own complicated positioning with regard to dominant representations of gender. Moreover, the specific form of this memory text opens up for discussion questions relating to genre, authorial intention, and authenticity.

Méndez's literary career spanned over fifty years, with the author publishing some ten volumes of poetry, together with several plays and film scripts, between 1926 and the early 1980s.[1] Her literary production as a poet and playwright, together with her central role in the publication of significant literary journals of the day, brought her a considerable degree of integration into the male-dominated cultural elite of pre–Civil War Madrid, as she developed important personal and professional links with key male writers of the period. Despite this, Méndez's position in relation to this group is marginal and peripheral. Like so many of her contemporaries, Méndez went into exile after the Spanish Civil War; she eventually settled in Mexico where she lived until her death in 1986.

Born into a middle-class family in Madrid, Méndez's upbringing and education were typical for a young woman of her social class in early twentieth-century Spain. She received a traditional gender-structured education, designed to prepare young girls for their fu-

118

ture roles as wives and mothers. Nevertheless, Méndez indicates her disconformity from an early age with conventional gender prescriptions. Forbidden from reading and writing, the young Méndez began to write at night when her parents were asleep, creating a tale of an imaginary journey (Méndez 1990, 28). Méndez's interest in both travel and writing continued into her adolescent years, and she also participated in unconventional physical activities, outside the bounds of the traditionally "feminine," such as swimming and athletics. The 1920s was a particularly critical period in Méndez's life: during this decade, she published her first volumes of poetry, was involved in the founding of the Lyceum Club, and traveled abroad against her family's wishes. This latter act signals Méndez's definitive rejection of the bourgeois values represented by her family, who deemed her interests to be inappropriate for a woman. Méndez later asserts that she felt like an "extranjera" [foreigner] (1990, 87) in her family environment; while she and her father broke off contact, Méndez and her mother did retain minimal contact in later years.

During this period, Méndez also began to associate with a select circle of writers, artists, and intellectuals who were to have a profound influence on the young poet. In fact, Méndez's memoirs, like León's, constitute something of a who's who of the literary and cultural scene of early twentieth-century Spain. In particular, Méndez developed close friendships with filmmaker Luis Buñuel, who was her boyfriend during her teenage years, Rafael Alberti, and Federico García Lorca. It was Lorca who introduced Méndez to poet Manuel Altolaguirre, whom she married in 1932 and with whom she had a daughter, Paloma.[2] During the 1920s, Méndez also produced her first volumes of poetry, *Inquietudes* [Restlessness] (1926) and *Surtidor* [Fountain] (1928), publications that marked the beginning of a decade of prolific literary activity for Méndez as she enjoyed the stimulating creative environment of pre–Civil War Madrid. In fact, between 1926 and the outbreak of the war, Méndez published five volumes of poetry, four dramatic works, and a film script, as well as a number of articles in literary journals. In addition to their individual writing, Méndez and Altolaguirre together published a number of literary journals and collections of poetry, setting up a small printing press at home. Moreover, in the years leading up to the outbreak of the Civil War, the couple's home in Madrid became an important meeting place for many of the writers of the period.[3]

While political issues are not at the forefront of Méndez's poetic or autobiographical works, the political context of 1930s Spain was nevertheless decisive for her literary career. Like so many writers and artists of the period, Méndez was a supporter of the Republic, despite professing no affiliation to any specific political party. As was noted in earlier chapters of this study, the political turmoil of the years of the Second Republic and the Civil War, together with the changing social and gender dynamics of these years, brought unprecedented levels of participation by women in a wide range of cultural activities. During the war years, both Méndez and Altolaguirre participated in the Republican war effort, with Méndez writing news reports to send overseas and Altolaguirre continuing his work as a printer.

Following the Republican defeat in the conflict, the couple and their young daughter sought refuge with friends in France, before traveling to Cuba and, four years later, settling in Mexico. The hardship, both emotional and financial, of life in exile is evident in both Méndez's poetry of the decade following the war and in her memoirs. This was a particularly difficult period in the author's life: in addition to experiencing the trauma of exile, Méndez was faced with the end of her marriage when Altolaguirre left her for another woman. Furthermore, the rupture with her homeland necessitated by the Republican defeat in the Civil War meant not only exile from her country of birth, but also from the literary center.

After the war, Méndez fell into oblivion and disappeared from most literary records in Spain. While many writers of her generation, male and female, found themselves in a similar situation, the effect of exile on male poets was less severe; as Bellver notes, "[w]hile most men were eventually reintegrated into the literary consciousness, women poets were virtually obliterated" (2001, 26). While Méndez never permanently relocated to her homeland, she did make a number of trips back to Spain before her death. It is significant that on her return visits to Spain in the late 1960s Méndez was finally recognized and acclaimed as a pioneer by members of her family, indicative of the quite different social and ideological context of the late Franco years. Méndez does not make any specific political comment when recounting in *Memorias* her trips to her homeland, despite the fact that the regime from which she fled remained in power.

Memorias habladas, memorias armadas is the result of a collaborative project undertaken by Méndez and her granddaughter, Paloma Ulacia Altolaguirre, in the 1980s. While the text is a first-person account of Méndez's life story, this is not an autobiography according to traditional definitions of the genre. The work itself was compiled by Ulacia, based on twenty-three hours of recordings with her grandmother, which she then edited, a process that invites an examination of the text in light of theories of oral history.

Defined by David Henige as "the study of the recent past by means of life histories or personal recollections, where informants speak about their own experiences" (1982, 2), oral history has been hailed by critics as a means of providing a history "from below" that gives voice to the unprivileged and, as a result, challenges socially coded binary oppositions such as public/private, literacy/orality, and high/low culture.[4] Within the Hispanic context, the form of narrative text that has come to be known as the *testimonio* similarly gives voice to those silenced by cultural or political hegemonies. However, in his work on the *testimonio,* critic John Beverley distinguishes this form from oral history, emphasizing that the narrator of the former seeks specifically to testify or bear witness to a particular experience, and that it is this individual's desire to communicate his or her story that is primary in a *testimonio:* "In oral history, it is the intentionality of the recorder . . . that is dominant, and the resulting text is in some sense 'data.' In *testimonio,* by contrast, it is the intentionality of the narrator that is paramount" (1992, 94). In the case of Méndez's text, the intentionality of both narrator and recorder come through strongly in the text and of particular significance is the fact that these coincide, as is discussed below.

It is important to bear in mind that the *testimonio,* a narrative form designated an "out-law" genre by Caren Kaplan (1992), has been seen to be closely aligned with political struggles and with the representation of a collective social situation and it is, moreover, particularly associated with the Latin American context. However, Dupláa has argued that the concept of *testimonio* can also be relevant to works produced by European writers, signaling that "the *marginality* and *peripheral nature* of the testimonial voice is also found in European cultures that have suffered linguistic and cultural impositions, whether from within or outside their national borders" (1996, 13; italics in original). Both oral history and the *testimonio,* then, seek to give voice to the subaltern—those on the periphery of a given cultural, social, or political arena—albeit through the intermediary of a recorder or writer.

As an educated, middle-class woman and as a writer, Méndez is not the typical subject of oral history nor of the *testimonio,* and the imbalances in power and privilege between the narrator and the interviewer which characterize many oral history projects are clearly not applicable to Méndez and Ulacia. However, in addition to meth-odological associations, *Memorias* is aligned in other ways with the practice of oral history, particularly if, with Paul Thompson, we adopt the notion that oral history can constitute "a means for trans-forming both the content and the purpose of history" (1988, 2). In this work, Méndez undeniably seeks to challenge established ver-sions of history and to inscribe herself in historical and literary re-cords from which she has been excluded. Moreover, Méndez inevitably writes or speaks from a subaltern position in a patriarchal society. I am not, however, proposing here that *Memorias* be desig-nated a *testimonio* or oral history, as Méndez's text diverges from these forms in many respects. I seek, rather, to signal the way in which critical work in this area may shed light on the specific form this text takes and on the role played by Ulacia in its production and reception.

It is clear that Ulacia's role in producing *Memorias* goes well be-yond that of a transcriber. While it is widely accepted that no auto-biographical text can be strictly referential of a life and that such writing inevitably involves a process of selection, in this case that process is double, as first Méndez, and then Ulacia, shape the form and content of the text. This duality, typical of a *testimonio* or oral history project, is indicated in the title of the text, *Memorias habladas, memorias armadas,* which refers to the way in which the memories of the past recounted therein are spoken by Méndez and assembled by Ulacia.

Ulacia indicates in her prologue an awareness of the selective as-pect of the writing process, referring both to her grandmother's ten-dency to omit or gloss over more painful memories from her past—"su voluntad por ir seleccionando los hechos" [her wish to go through selecting the facts] (1990, 18)—and to the fact that her own task in producing the text involved both selection and reconstruc-tion. Likening this process to the completion of a jigsaw puzzle—"como aquel que arma un rompecabezas, me puse a extraer las piezas importantes y a unirlas" [like someone assembling a jigsaw puzzle, I started to extract the important pieces and bring them to-gether] (1990, 20)—Ulacia is careful to clarify that only superfluous material was omitted during this process, giving a specific example of a family anecdote that she chose to leave out (1990, 21) and em-phasizing that she carried out the transcription and editing work "de manera minuciosa, respetando en lo posible los giros idiomát-icos de mi abuela" [in a detailed manner, respecting wherever possible the idiomatic twists of my grandmother] (1990, 20). Ulacia goes on to assure the reader that her grandmother's intentions in narrating her life story were respected, noting that the final version of the memoirs was approved by Méndez, who had the complete text read to her and had the opportunity to make corrections (1990, 21). Ulacia's detailed description of the writing process points to her awareness of the problematics of being perceived to "speak for others" and of the anxiety caused by collaborative works such as *Memorias,* as signaled by Lejeune: "The division of labor between two people . . . reveals the multiplicity of authorities implied in the work of autobiographical writing, as in all writing" (1989, 186).

This collaborative form deployed by Méndez and Ulacia thus invokes questions regarding intention—the authorial motive governing the production of the text, as noted above in the discussion of oral history and *testimonio*—as well as issues of textual authenticity: that is, the "truth" status of the work in relation to the fact/fiction dichotomy. These two issues are raised in Ulacia's affirmation in her prologue that Méndez, through their collaborative text, sought to assert that "aunque nadie lo creyera, al igual que Luis Cernuda, o García Lorca, o Manuel Altolaguirre, ella también había tenido una experiencia vital interesante" [although nobody may have believed it, just like Luis Cernuda, or García Lorca, or Manuel Altolaguirre, she, too, had had an interesting life experience] (1990, 18). Significant here is the suggestion that Méndez doubts that her account of the past will be believed, a point reiterated by Ulacia's observation that to her grandmother's new social circle in Mexico, Méndez's experiences "sonaban como arte de su fantasía, más que de su experiencia" [sounded more like the workings of her imagination than her experience] (1990, 15). This raises the question of the role of "truth" in life-writing and the perceived need for the writer to attest constantly to the authenticity of his or her account.

While critics generally concur that accuracy of recall is less important than a sincere intention on the part of the writer to achieve autobiographical veracity—in itself, a difficult element to evaluate—Méndez's exclusion from literary history makes her particularly determined to affirm the truth status of her account of the past. In this vein, Méndez makes reference on a number of occasions to letters and documents that would serve to corroborate her account but that she is unable to provide, due to the events of the war and her subsequent exile. For example, in reference to letters sent to her by Alberti, Méndez offers the following explanation: "Aquellas cartas, juntas con otras ilustradas de Federico [García Lorca], las tenía guardadas en una caja de banco, que perdí en la guerra" [Those letters, together with other, illustrated ones from Federico (García Lorca), I kept in a bank deposit box which was lost in the war] (1990, 56–57). Méndez thus suggests that access to such documents would validate her narrative, indicating her awareness of the way in which the written word holds a privileged position in terms of authenticity. As an oral account, her reflections may be perceived to be less significant and credible.

This anxiety on the part of Méndez regarding the credibility of her account means that, unlike Ulacia, she does not acknowledge memory as a process, making few references to the autobiographical process in the text. In fact, Méndez refutes the idea that she is producing an autobiography as such: "Pienso sólo en contar anécdotas y no en buscar una interpretación de mi vida" [I intend only to tell anecdotes and not to seek an interpretation of my life] (1990, 33). Such a description of her work is, in a sense, quite accurate, given the oral nature of her account; the chronology and coherence of *Memorias* was imposed later by Ulacia. It is, however, an interpretation of her life story which she ultimately produces, whether intentionally or not, a fact suggested by the final lines of the memoirs in which Méndez affirms that through the process of speaking about her past she has given form to her life (1990, 150).

While the specific form of this work is atypical of life-writing, the involvement of a second person as transcriber or cowriter of a life story is similarly seen in a number of other autobiographical works by Spanish women that were published in the late twentieth century, as Caballé has signaled. This technique, Caballé hypothesizes, indicates that these women needed from the interviewer "a final push that made them decide to cross the frontiers of intimacy" (1998, 127). While the initiative for recording and publishing Méndez's life story does appear to have been Ulacia's, she signals that she was motivated to do so by her grandmother's desire to remember and recount her past (1990, 17–18). In addition, Ulacia notes that there was a physical consideration also: Méndez's failing eyesight meant that she was unable to write her memoirs herself (1990, 18).

The motivation for producing *Memorias* for both Méndez and Ulacia is, then, a desire to inscribe Concha Méndez into Spain's literary history, alongside her male contemporaries of the 1920s, specifically the famed members of the "Generation of 1927." Through her oral account of her life story, Méndez speaks out to set the record straight regarding her role as a writer and intellectual who participated in the literary scene of early twentieth-century Spain. This intentionality is made explicit by Ulacia's affirmation that "[a] través de estas memorias, [Méndez] quería regresar a España y encontrar el lugar que le correspondía dentro de la historia literaria de su país" [through these memoirs, (Méndez) wanted to return to Spain and find her rightful place within the literary history of her country] (1990, 22). Critics have echoed Ulacia's call for Méndez to be recognized as a significant figure in Spanish literary history. Hence Cole affirms that Méndez played "an important role in developing the feminine voice of the Generation of 1927" (2000, 138), while Pérez notes that she figures "among Spain's more significant women poets of exile" (1996, 58). Mangini, too, attributes her a place as "an integral member of that movement of friends and collaborators" (2001, 179).

The reason for Méndez's exclusion from the literary canon is attributed by Ulacia to "la misoginia de sus contemporáneos" [the misogyny of her contemporaries] (1990, 16), and she makes specific reference to her grandmother's exclusion from Gerardo Diego's well-known anthology. The sometimes ambivalent, if not overtly negative, reaction of Méndez's male contemporaries to her literary and cultural contributions are evident in their own personal writings (memoirs and letters, for example) and in published interviews from the period in question. Some of these texts fail to mention Méndez at all, while in other instances her intellectual role as a fellow writer is granted minimal attention, as she is instead depicted as a maternal figure or as a negative and disruptive influence on Altolaguirre.[5] Such attitudes were expressed by writers and intellectuals with whom Méndez had close social relationships and with whom she collaborated in a professional sense, confirming the following observation made by Bellver: "Paradoxically some of the critics, writers, and intellectuals with whom women writers maintained cordial personal and professional relationships made some of the most negative comments on them" (1997a, 213).

In *Memorias,* it is her connections with the male writers and intellectuals who comprise the "Generation of 1927" that Méndez foregrounds, as she emphasizes her involvement in the cultural and literary scene of the period and thus suggests that she should be inserted into literary history alongside her contemporaries. She indicates, moreover, that the editorial work that she undertook together with Altolaguirre was instrumental in the actual formation of the

"Generation," affirming that without the existence of such publications as *Héroe* and *1616* "no se hubiese podido crear una unidad de grupo" [it would not have been possible to create group unity] (1990, 92). Such an emphasis on the importance of group unity as a defining feature of the "Generation of 1927" replicates traditional formulations of the literary generation, highlighting also the way in which publications and literary promotion contribute to canon creation. Furthermore, Méndez does fulfill a number of the criteria traditionally adopted by literary critics for membership of the so-called "generation." Born in 1898, her birth date falls within the range of 1891 and 1905 generally accepted by critics;[6] she published her first two volumes of poetry, *Inquietudes* and *Surtidor,* in 1926 and 1928 respectively, years that saw the publication of key works by members of the "generation"; and in her poetry, Méndez deployed many of the poetic techniques used by her male contemporaries, as well as expressing similar thematic concerns.

The connections between Méndez's work and that of male poets of the 1920s have, however, been seen as a negative factor by some critics, who have dismissed her poetry as mere imitation of works by other writers, particularly those of her mentor, Alberti (Mainer 1989, 22, 25). The influence of Alberti on Méndez's early works is indisputable, and she confirms his key role in supporting her early poetic endeavors in her memoirs: "Rafael y yo empezamos a citarnos, para leer nuestras cosas . . . Me explicaba lo que era una metáfora o una imagen" [Rafael and I began to meet in order to read our works . . . He explained to me what a metaphor or an image was] (1990, 47). Despite this influence, Méndez is nevertheless successful in projecting her own voice in her poetry, diverging from masculine models in certain respects, as Bellver has convincingly argued in her analyses of Méndez's work (1997b, 2001). It is, in fact, this element of Méndez's work that is emphasized by Wilcox, who foregrounds the "gynocentric" nature of Méndez's poetry, which, he argues, positions her outside the androcentric canon (1997, 87–133).

The debate surrounding the originality or otherwise of Méndez's work is an example of the overwhelming difficulties placed in the paths of women attempting to establish themselves in a male-dominated literary culture: on the one hand, if their works conform to male models, they are criticized for lacking creativity and originality; if, on the other hand, their works break with models of the time, they are deemed to fall outside dominant literary tradition and thus outside the canon.

While there is, then, evidence to support the claim made by Ulacia and by some contemporary critics that Méndez rightly belongs in the so-called "Generation of 1927," the value of perpetuating the use of such generational concepts is questionable, as was argued in the first chapter of this study. Expanding the canon to include female poets, as Cole has advocated (2000, 176), achieves some modification to the masculine historical record—as per Lerner's concept of "contribution history" (1976, 358)—but does not propose a fundamental revision of the prevailing hegemonic models. This is, however, the stance adopted by Méndez and Ulacia in *Memorias*. As they undermine the notion of the "Generation of 1927" by articulating its shortcomings and omissions, they simultaneously affirm its existence and seek to uphold it, albeit in a revised, expanded version. It is, of course, only by validating the canon that Méndez may partake of its recognized prestige.

As such, it is precisely her participation in the intellectual practices of the canonical "generation" that Méndez foregrounds in *Memorias*. In particular, she positions her own home with Altolaguirre as one of the key centers of their cultural activities, as she repeatedly makes reference to the regular visits to their home of well-known writers and intellectuals, to their *tertulias,* and to their interest in the printing work carried out in the couple's flat: "Todos los días se volcaban en la habitación los poetas de la generación del 27: Cernuda, Aleixandre, Lorca y otros; venían a vernos y a ver las revistas que nosotros imprimíamos con cosas suyas" [Every day the poets of the Generation of 1927 created uproar in the room: Cernuda, Aleixandre, Lorca, and others; they came to see us and to see the journals in which we were printing their works] (1990, 87). Méndez thus positions both herself and her home as pivotal to the generation, as she depicts the domestic realm of her home as an intellectual space that she shares with men, in opposition to traditional conceptions of the domestic as the domain of women, antithetical to the "masculine" cultural world.

Méndez's depiction of her home as an important site of intellectual and cultural practice for the writers of the "Generation of 1927" is confirmed in the portrait of the period presented by Carlos Morla Lynch in his diary. Significantly, however, Méndez herself is all but absent in this account. The Méndez-Altolaguirre home is constructed by Morla Lynch as a male-dominated space, much as it is in

Méndez's own account, but here it is presented as the domain of Altolaguirre (or "Manolito"), with Méndez herself absent or on the periphery: "Manolito's print shop is assuming the character of an intimate literary center where all the poets of the day and their friends gather" (1958, 236). Likewise, while Morla Lynch notes the significance of the printing ventures undertaken in the couple's home, he presents these as tasks taken on solely by Altolaguirre, noting that the poet "prepares there exquisite editions with impeccable presentation. The task he has taken on must be overwhelming" (1958, 235). While he does go on to mention Méndez's role in the publication of the literary journal *Héroe,* he describes her contribution in the following terms: "Concha Méndez, with the actions of a strong young man and with magnificent agility, moves levers, places and removes papers, and tightens screws" (1958, 241). It is thus Méndez's physical, rather than intellectual, contribution that Morla Lynch emphasizes, presenting her as a laborer on the project and making reference to her use of the workman's *mono azul* [blue overalls]. While the physical labor undertaken by Méndez that Morla Lynch describes is nonconventional for a woman, his description of her contribution is nevertheless in a sense in accordance with patriarchal ideology, in terms of its association of woman with the body, rather than with intellect, deemed to be the preserve of men.

Significantly, Méndez likewise emphasizes her physical role in the operation of the printing press, noting the strength required to operate the machinery and making reference to the masculine clothing she wore while working: "Era yo quien la manejaba; la manejaba vestida con un mono azul de mecánico; era difícil y cansado, pero como era deportista, tenía una fuerza increíble" [It was I who operated the machinery; I operated it dressed in a mechanic's blue overalls; it was difficult and tiring, but as I was a sportswoman, I had incredible strength] (1990, 87). Later, she similarly positions herself as a laborer, indicating moreover a clear division of roles between herself and Altolaguirre: "[É]l era el tipógrafo; y yo, vestida de mecánico, la fuerza que hacía girar la imprenta" [He was the typesetter; and I, dressed as a mechanic, the force that caused the press to turn] (1990, 93). Hence Altolaguirre, as typographer, is attributed less status: he merely set the letters, while it was Méndez's efforts that actually produced the publications. Of relevance here with regard to Méndez's emphasis on her donning of the workman's overalls is the fact that some of the male writers of this period wore the workman's *mono azul* as a means of expressing solidarity with the working classes, with the use of this garment thus assuming a political dimension. By wearing the *mono azul,* Méndez thus violates boundaries of both gender and class.

In this section of her memoirs, Méndez thus narrates her adoption of a masculine role and apparel to further highlight her central role in the literary endeavors of this male-dominated group and to emphasize her alignment with her male peers. However, while Méndez's text suggests that this masculinization of her identity enables her to gain acceptance and credibility within the "generation," she simultaneously notes that, outside this intellectual community, her unconventional approach increased her marginalization. Méndez affirms, for example, that "la gente se quedaba extrañadísima" [people found it very strange] when she wore her laborer's overalls in public (1990, 87).

Despite this negative reaction to her "unfeminine" appearance, Méndez's memoirs make it clear that the writer is proud of her attempts to transcend the gendered norms that prevail in this sociohistorical context. Her reference here to the uniqueness of her experience in a traditionally masculine environment is one of several instances in the memoirs where she emphasizes her singularity, positioning herself as something of a pioneer. In addition to her claim of being perhaps the only woman in Madrid to wear trousers (1990, 87), Méndez similarly affirms that she was one of the few women who traveled alone (1990, 72), one of only a small number of women writers who had works published in Spain (1990, 54), and the only writer among the Lyceum Club members (1990, 49).[7] This awareness of the transgressive nature of her life story is not purely a result of her intervening experience or of the memory process that culminates in her recordings in the 1980s; in an interview conducted in 1930, Méndez similarly affirmed that she considered herself to be "en las filas de una doble vanguardia, por lo que se refiere al Arte y a la Sociedad" [in the ranks of a double vanguard, by which is meant both Art and Society] (quoted in Valender 2001c, 52). Méndez thus consciously positions and writes herself as an exceptional figure whose life experiences are unique and atypical, although she simultaneously seeks to represent her full integration as a "normal" member of the male-dominated literary community of her day.

This apparent contradiction in Méndez's memoirs points to what Melissa Dinverno has termed the "dueling projects" of the Méndez-Ulacia text: a critique of the marginalization of women intellectuals and the legitimation of Méndez as a writer (2003, 68).[8] In this respect, then, the memoir is paradoxical, as Méndez appears to take issue with the gendered literary system, while simultaneously seeking legitimation from it and replicating its exclusionary politics. This paradox is, for example, apparent in Méndez's discussions of the literary journal *Héroe,* which she and Altolaguirre produced. In this section of her memoirs, Méndez emphasizes the importance of this publication, as was mentioned above, but she significantly downplays the contributions of her female peers. In this way, Méndez replicates the stance adopted by other writers, such as Morla Lynch. Affirming the importance of *Héroe* and stating that "the whole pleiad of youthful stars" were to participate in the publication (1958, 236), Morla Lynch goes on to name the canonical figures of the "Generation of 1927" such as Altolaguirre, Cernuda, Lorca, Aleixandre, and Alberti as contributors to the journal. Neither Méndez nor any of her female contemporaries who certainly did publish in *Héroe* are mentioned.

While Morla Lynch's omission of women writers from his discussion of *Héroe* is perhaps unsurprising, given the widespread tendency for their contribution to be overlooked, what is significant is that this neglect should be perpetuated in Méndez's own text. While she does note that a number of women figure in *Héroe,* these writers are nevertheless excluded from her conception of the "generation": the literary center represented by Méndez in her memoirs appears to be constituted by the male writers who are at the forefront of intellectual activity at the time, together with Méndez herself. Her female contemporaries are aligned in her account, not with their male contemporaries of the "Generation of 1927," but with foreign writers: "Sacamos seis números de la revista *Héroe.* En ella no sólo incluimos a los poetas de la generación, sino también a Rosa Chacel, Ernestina de Champourcín y a varios escritores extranjeros" [We brought out six issues of the journal *Héroe.* In it we included not only the poets of the Generation, but also Rosa Chacel, Ernestina de Champourcín, and various foreign writers] (1990, 93). Thus in Méndez's own presentation of the literary scene of 1920s and 1930s Madrid, women are presented as on the periphery, marginal to the intellectual world dominated by men.

The general lack of attention paid by Méndez to her female contemporaries in *Memorias* is interesting, for she was without question in contact with other female writers and artists. In fact, Mangini affirms that Ernestina de Champourcín and María Teresa León were among those who participated in the regular gatherings at the home of Méndez and Altolaguirre, and also notes that Méndez dedicates poems in the volume *Canciones de mar y tierra* [Songs of the Sea and Earth] (1930) to many other *modernas* (2001, 164–65, 172). In addition, Méndez developed a friendship with María Zambrano, who was among the guests at Méndez's wedding and who, nearly sixty years later, wrote an introduction to Méndez's memoirs.

The one friendship which the author does present as particularly influential is that which she developed with artist Maruja Mallo, who was a key figure in Méndez's radical break with her family and their social circle. She also makes reference to other women with whom she established contact, including members of the Lyceum Club such as Zenobia de Camprubí and Pilar de Zubiaurre. However, these friendships and the intellectual and cultural ties among women are presented as very much secondary in *Memorias*. It may well be that Méndez considered these relationships to be less important than those that she developed with her male contemporaries, who were very influential in both her professional and private life. It nevertheless seems likely that Méndez consciously chose not to foreground these friendships, in an attempt to further emphasize her affinity with her male counterparts. In this way, Méndez distances herself from the separate space occupied by women writers and artists, deemed to be inherently inferior, and highlights her own exceptionality.

One of the attempts at creating a networking opportunity for women intellectuals in 1920s Madrid which Méndez does discuss is the Lyceum Club, although the author's positioning in relation to this organization in *Memorias* is complex. While she signals the importance of the association as a women's cultural center, emphasizing her own involvement in its establishment, Méndez nevertheless expresses some criticisms of the Club, suggesting an awareness of the limitations of such an association in that specific sociohistorical context. She notes her own description of some of the Lyceum Club members as "maridas de sus maridos" [husbandettes] (1990, 49), a reference to the perceived lack of intellectual independence of some of her contemporaries, specifically those who were the wives of famous men.[9] Méndez's affirmation that these women's participation in the discussions at the Lyceum was limited to repeating their husbands' views—"venían a la tertulia a contar lo que habían oído en casa" [they came to the gathering to tell us what they had heard at home] (1990, 49)—calls into question the ability of this institution to achieve its goal of creating a space "where women could exchange ideas without the interference of men" (Bellver 2001, 35). Méndez's depiction of the *tertulias* suggests that male voices and discourse did, in fact, penetrate the supposedly female domain of the Lyceum Club, and she also notes that some of the Club's members did not participate in the discussions at all.[10] Méndez affirms, moreover, that she was the youngest member of the Club and the only writer, again suggesting a distance between herself and her contemporaries and perhaps even alluding to a certain superiority on her part in intellectual terms. Méndez's assertion that she was the only writer in the Lyceum Club is, of course, inaccurate; writers such as Isabel Oyarzábal de Palencia, Carmen Conde, and María Teresa León were also members. While it is possible that Méndez was unaware that her fellow members were writers, it seems more likely that this is simply one of the omissions or distortions that characterize memory writing. Conversely, this may be a conscious omission to highlight further Méndez's role as a "pioneer."

Her criticisms of the Lyceum Club notwithstanding, Méndez does acknowledge that this organization brought her into contact with people who, she affirms, "me abrían las puertas a una realidad que favorecía mi espíritu" [opened for me the doors to a reality that favored my spirit] (1990, 50). Moreover, she emphasizes the importance of the Lyceum Club as a center of cultural and intellectual engagement for women: "[S]obre todo era un centro cultural; tenía bibliotecas y un salón para espectáculos y conferencias" [Above all it was a cultural center; it had libraries and a reception room for performances and lectures] (1990, 49). It is thus the merit of the Lyceum Club as a physical space for the advancement of women which Méndez highlights.

It is precisely the lack of such a space in which to pursue intellectual interests which Méndez encounters early on in her literary career. Unable to write at home, lacking, quite literally, a "room of her own" in which to create, Méndez affirms that she wrote many of her early works on park benches (1990, 47), in the fields behind her parent's home (1990, 61), and "en las sillas que no roba nadie de los paseos en Madrid" [on the seats that nobody steals from the avenues of Madrid] (1990, 53). The young Méndez was, moreover, "retired" from school by her parents at the age of fourteen, finding herself in what she describes as "un desierto" [a desert] (1990, 28) in which she had to resort to deception to read and write. Later, Méndez was similarly prohibited from attending university; in fact, her attendance at a single lecture led her mother to punish her physically

(1990, 45). Furthermore, Méndez was unable to attend evening *tertulias*, a further crucial space for intellectual activity and stimulation in this context, as she was obliged to return home for dinner (1990, 59–60). Emphasizing the limitations, both physical and psychological, of the domestically focused life prescribed for her—"no podía moverme si no iba custodiada por alguien" [I was unable to move unless I was in somebody's custody] (1990, 45)—Méndez repeatedly reveals how this life ensured her exclusion from the intellectual world in which she aspired to participate. The clearly demarcated gender roles and the concomitant separation of male and female spheres in the sociohistorical context represented by Méndez is thus shown to impede women's participation in cultural endeavors.[11]

Such a separation is made explicit in *Memorias* by Méndez's description of her seven-year relationship with Luis Buñuel, whom she describes as living a "doble vida" [double life] (1990, 40), in which his life with his girlfriend was totally separate from his intellectual life, centered around the male space of the Residencia de Estudiantes. Noting that such a separation was customary at the time, Méndez nevertheless signals her resentment at her exclusion, referring to the rich intellectual world of the Residencia as "todo lo que viví sin vivir durante años" [everything that I lived for years without living it] (1990, 46). Méndez's account makes it clear that, while Buñuel did not introduce her to any of his friends nor invite her to their gatherings, he did talk to her about his activities at the Residencia and about his friends, and she notes a comment made by her chaperone that the young couple are "extrañísimos" [exceedingly strange] due to their unconventional topics of conversation during their social outings (1990, 39).[12]

In this section of her text, Méndez indicates the importance of these glimpses of Buñuel's "other life" for her own awareness of an alternative to the bourgeois routines of her life with her family: "Y yo, en el inconsciente, seguramente me iba enterando de la posibilidad de otro mundo, que no fuera la familia, los hermanitos" [And I, in my unconscious, began to find out about the possibility of another world that was not my family, my younger siblings] (1990, 39). Méndez thus presents her teenage relationship with Buñuel as formative in terms of the future direction of her own life, signaling the way in which her role as his girlfriend enabled her to gain access to this other world in which he moved, evidenced by her affirmation in an interview with Max Aub that "para mí fueron muy interesantes las relaciones con Buñuel, me sirvieron para conocer luego a la gente de la Residencia" [for me my relationship with Buñuel was very interesting, and later enabled me to meet people from the Residencia] (quoted in Aub 1985, 243). Moreover, Méndez used these connections with Buñuel strategically even after their relationship had ended and he had moved to Paris; in her memoirs she reveals that she consciously exploited her position as his former girlfriend as a way of meeting Lorca and thus making contact with other writers and artists associated with the Residencia, such as Alberti and Altolaguirre, by phoning the Residencia on the pretext of asking after Buñuel's health (1990, 46). Méndez thus presents herself as constantly resisting the barriers designed to exclude her from the intellectual world. While the memoirs narrate some successes on Méndez's part in this regard—she does, after all, meet Lorca and her future mentor Alberti in this way—it is overall a disheartening panorama that she presents, as she repeatedly highlights what she describes as "el desaliento de mi medio ambiente" [the dispiriting nature of my environment] (1990, 41).

These restrictions were, of course, obstacles encountered by Méndez before her definitive break with her family, when she herself was forced to lead a form of "double life," "moviéndome en los dos mundos" [circulating within two worlds] (1990, 57). It is without doubt a more positive environment from a creative and intellectual standpoint that she enjoyed later with Altolaguirre, despite Biruté Ciplijauskaité's affirmation that, for both Méndez and Champourcin, marriage constituted their "voluntary exile from a total concentration in their fulfillment as artists" (1989, 121), and a precursor to their physical exile of 1939. Ciplijauskaité's suggestion that the fact that the women poets of the 1920s were married to members of Madrid's literary elite further contributed to their marginalization is echoed by Wilcox, who similarly affirms that they were seen only as the wives of poets, rather than as literary figures in their own right (1994, 292). However, while Méndez certainly did not achieve the canonical status of Altolaguirre, her relationship with him did result in a greater integration into the literary scene than she may otherwise have achieved. Moreover, in contrast to Ciplijauskaité's thesis that Méndez's marriage had an adverse effect on her commitment to her literary career, other critics signal that, in fact, Méndez produced her best and most mature poetic works during the twelve years of her marriage to Altolaguirre (Valender 2001b, 63; Quance 2001, 111–12). Roberta Quance attributes this not only to Altolaguirre's influence on Méndez, but also to the more favorable conditions enjoyed by women writers during the years of the Republic, a period characterized by more liberal cultural and sexual politics and the quest for modernity in all areas of society. In *Memorias,* it is precisely her experiences as a female intellectual in "modern" Spain that Méndez recounts.

Born, as she affirms in *Memorias,* "en medio de la modernidad" [in the midst of modernity] (1990, 29), Méndez is in many respects the epitome of the women whom Mangini denominates "las modernas de Madrid" [the modern women of Madrid] (2001). While, like some of her contemporaries, she does not explicitly position herself as a feminist in her memoirs—echoing her 1928 affirmation that "yo no sé si soy feminista o no" [I do not know whether I am a feminist or not] (quoted in Valender 2001c, 35)—Méndez's work does reveal aspects of her feminist vision in terms of her denunciation of the limitations imposed on women in early twentieth-century Spain. Noting with chagrin that in legal terms a married woman in Spain was considered equivalent to a child or a person suffering from mental illness (1990, 68), Méndez nevertheless acknowledges her lack of attention to issues pertaining to the social situation of women in her literary works, specifically her plays, a fact that she herself deems "curioso" [curious] (1990, 95). That Méndez did not focus on issues specifically pertaining to women may be read as a further element in her attempts to distance herself from the "feminine" and to position herself within the bounds of the masculine literary center.

In addition to her disconformity with gender norms and her developing interests in culture and politics, Méndez's participation in a range of sporting activities, such as athletics, tennis, and swimming competitions, firmly positions her as a "modern" woman in the context of early twentieth-century Spain. Moreover, references to the technological advances of the first decades of the century—"aviadores, aviones, motores, hélices, telecomunicaciones" [aviators, aircraft, motors, propellers, telecommunications] (1990, 29)—abound in Méndez's memoirs, as well as in her early poetry. Closely associated with such images of modernity is Méndez's description of the city of Madrid, as she makes reference to the changes that occur in the urban landscape during the period in question and narrates the ways in which she formulates her identity as a female intellectual in this changing urban environment.

Recent scholarship has produced an emerging body of research on feminist issues relating to gender and the urban environment.[13]

Premised on the recognition that men's and women's experiences in and perceptions of the city are different, work in this area of urban studies has explored the constraints that affect women's lives in an urban space. While Elizabeth Wilson writes of the city as a potential "place of liberation for women," noting that "[the] city offers women freedom" (1991, 7), she nevertheless recognizes that women often do not have full and free access to the streets and other crucial sites of the urban environment. It is such a dual relationship with the city of Madrid that Méndez depicts in *Memorias,* as she represents the ways in which she assimilated city culture, while indicating that certain aspects of urban life are off-limits for women.

The urban environment of 1920s and 1930s Madrid, outside the limited literary community of which Méndez considered herself a part, is presented in *Memorias* as generally hostile and restrictive for women who sought to venture beyond the domestic sphere. Denied access to certain places, such as taverns and the other venues at which *tertulias* were held, and with specific streets and neighborhoods deemed to be inappropriate for women to frequent, Méndez nevertheless describes her refusal to conform to such limitations. In the company of Lorca and Alberti, she walks down the Calle Sevilla, despite the fact that "[s]e suponía que por esta calle no podían pasar las muchachas decentes" [it was supposed that decent young women could not walk along this street] (1990, 50), and with Mallo she visits Madrid's "barrios bajos" [low-class suburbs] (1990, 51), areas of the city that fall outside the limits of bourgeois society. In addition, Méndez and Mallo scandalize upper-middle-class Madrid by appearing in public without hats (1990, 48), and they press their faces to the windows of the taverns from which they are banned in a gesture that Méndez specifically writes as an act of protest (1990, 51). In this way, Méndez depicts herself as making the city hers despite the prevailing restrictions, and as reveling in the modernity that is developing all around her in Madrid.

Many of the modern innovations to which Méndez refers in her memoirs are in the area of transportation and new technologies of motion, of particular interest to her given her professed early interest in geography and maps and desire to see the world (1990, 28). The increased access to mobility in the first decades of the twentieth century is linked to changes in social relations and to the emergence of new kinds of identities for women, reflected in the figure of the *mujer nueva* [new woman] in Spain, epitomized by Méndez.

Independent travel is, however, deemed to be an inappropriate activity for a young woman of Méndez's social class: her parents initially frustrated her plans to leave Spain and in the end she departed for England without their knowledge or permission, aware of the anomalous nature of her situation: "[E]n aquellos tiempos no se veía a ninguna chica que viajara sola" [In those days no young woman was ever seen traveling alone] (1990, 72). As a female traveler, then, Méndez trespassed upon a further constitutively masculine domain. The linkage between travel and masculine identity is made explicit by Janet Woolf, who argues that "the ideological gendering of travel (as male) both impedes female travel and renders problematic the self-definition of (and response to) women who *do* travel" (1993, 234; italics in original). Seeking though travel a respite from the constraints of femininity and social expectations, and from an environment that she described in a 1942 interview as "la asfixia del ambiente burgués que me rodeaba" [the asphyxia of the bourgeois atmosphere that surrounded me] (quoted in Valender 2001c, 71), Méndez presents travel as both a form of escape and a means of achieving independence (1990, 83).

In her exploration of the politics associated with the gendering of travel and the representation of such issues in women's travel narratives, Sidonie Smith notes that, for women of the early twentieth century, travel could result in "an empowerment that derived from the negotiation of cultural displacement" (2001, 17). By traveling to England and, later, to Argentina, Méndez achieves her stated goal of independence from her family, supporting herself initially through translation work and teaching Spanish, and later publishing her poems in newspapers and giving lectures. She thus successfully negotiates her cultural displacement, engaging in the literary circles of Buenos Aires, an environment which Méndez presents as stimulating and nurturing for the female intellectual.

In this respect, Méndez's portrayal of her experiences in the Argentinian capital in the late 1920s (1990, 72–82) stands in marked contrast to her representation of the Madrid literary community as a man's world. In this section of her memoirs, Méndez highlights the collaborative friendships that she developed with other women who were active on the cultural scene, such as Alfonsina Storni and Consuelo Berges. She also met the Argentinian artist Norah Borges, who was a well-known illustrator of literary journals and who provided the drawings for Méndez's *Canciones de mar y tierra,* published in 1930.[14] In Méndez's account, urban Buenos Aires is depicted as a positive environment for the woman writer: she had a space to write, sharing an office with Berges, and she depicts the mutual support that she and Berges, as well as other female friends and colleagues, offered each other as key to the intellectual stimulation and publishing success that they enjoyed during this period. Méndez thus narrates in her memoirs the existence of a network of female intellectuals in Buenos Aires and the resulting sense of solidarity and community that, she appears to suggest, did not exist in Madrid at this time.

However, the "empowerment" referred to by Smith that Méndez may have derived from this positive experience of overseas travel is always limited by the fact that the hegemonic literary system with which she engaged was inherently masculine. This factor was particularly true of the environment of the 1930s Madrid to which she returned. It is also important to note that Méndez's later experiences of displacement were as an exiled subject, certainly not an experience of empowerment and a very different situation to the travel which she undertook in search of independence in the 1920s, when she was, in her words, "en voluntaria expatriación" [in voluntary exile] (quoted in Valender 2001c, 71).

Méndez's discussion of the political conditions that led to her enforced exile of the post–Civil War period reveal both her general sympathies with the Left and her rejection of specific political doctrines, such as communism and anarchism. While political concerns were not primary for writers in the 1920s and early 1930s, with the modernist credo described by critics as having been essentially apolitical, the events leading up to the outbreak of the Civil War meant that such a neutral stance was almost untenable.[15] There was thus a notable shift toward a more politically committed position on the part of writers, artists, and intellectuals of the period, as Nigel Dennis has noted: "The literary world became more politicized and divided as writers sought more radical and effective responses to changing circumstances" (2004, 574). Political and social issues thus took center stage at this time.

That the historical circumstances of the early 1930s signaled the definitive end of the *años felices* [happy years] of the 1920s is made explicit by Méndez in *Memorias:* "[T]oda la diversión se apagó; se apagaron las risas y los festejos, porque la situación en Madrid empezó a ponerse alarmante por la guerra" [All the entertainment was snuffed out; laughter and festivities were stifled, because the situation in Madrid began to become alarming, due to the war] (1990, 99). In addition, Méndez reveals that the political events did directly impact on the literary community in Madrid, noting that Alberti's affiliation with the Communist Party distances him from his peers, particularly when he included their names in a Communist manifesto without their permission (1990, 99).

While Méndez does not foreground her political views nor offer detailed analysis of the historical situation in her memoirs, she does offer her interpretation of the causes of the Civil War. Presenting the war as an international conflict between the extreme ideological positions represented by Nazism and Stalinism, Méndez posits Spain as the victim of external forces: "Por lo visto, España fue utilizada para discutir y plantear problemas ajenos a ella: por un lado, los nazis habían comprado a los militares encabezados por Franco, y por otro, se infiltró la ideología estalinista. Ellos pelearon entre sí y a nosotros nos confundieron" [It appears that Spain was used as a site to argue and raise other people's problems: on the one hand, the Nazis had bought the military, led by Franco, and on the other, there was infiltration of Stalinist ideology. They fought among themselves and they confused us] (1990, 100). Méndez thus emphasizes the external nature of the conflict, a reading of the war that contrasts with that put forward in recent studies; as James Cortada has noted, "modern-day interpretations of the causes of Spain's Civil War minimize international factors and stress purely internal Iberian forces" (1982, ix). Méndez's interpretation of the Spanish Civil War, formulated more than forty years after she left Spain and thus from the perspective of a long-term exile, seeks to downplay domestic conditions and the role of Spaniards themselves in the conflict. However, it is important to bear in mind that, unlike Martínez Sierra and León, Méndez was not a political activist: she does not claim to have expert knowledge of politics nor to present a precise historical account in her text.

As Méndez reflects in *Memorias* on the long years of exile that followed the Civil War, she highlights this period of her life as a time of intense isolation, particularly with regard to her years in Mexico. Her depictions of the four years that she and Altolaguirre spent together in Cuba, before settling in Mexico and prior to their separation, is more positive. In fact, Méndez's portrayal of this period evokes her earlier descriptions of the literary community in Madrid in the early 1930s, as she presents their home in Cuba as a meeting place for writers and intellectuals, including some well-known Latin American poets of the period. In addition, Méndez notes that in

Cuba she and Altolaguirre again operated a printing press to produce literary publications (1990, 110–11).

Méndez's representation of her experiences in Cuba as part of a literary community make her portrayal of the isolation of her life once she has settled in Coyoacán all the more marked. While this period is presented as productive in a literary sense, in that she is able to write, free of most of the restrictions she faced earlier in her life, Méndez's account highlights the way in which exile results in her displacement from the literary center. Méndez did not regularly participate in the *tertulias* or other gatherings associated with the literary establishment in Mexico, indicating a certain continuity in terms of her experience as a woman writer, always on the periphery of the cultural scene. Méndez's positioning in this regard in Mexico may be attributable, not only to her geopolitical exile, but also to the fact that by this time she was no longer the wife of Altolaguirre and had ceased to collaborate with him on literary ventures. Méndez thus no longer enjoyed the status that her former public identity as "wife of" a recognized literary figure inhered. Despite their separation, Méndez's memoirs reveal that she and Altolaguirre remained in close contact—she notes that her ex-husband visited her and her family regularly, commenting that "se fue y no se fue" [he went and he didn't go] (1990, 123) from her life—until Altolaguirre's death in 1959. For Méndez, the remaining years of her life as exiled subject in Mexico were dedicated to her house and garden, her family, and her writing.

From the standpoint of the woman writer in exile, *Memorias habladas, memorias armadas* articulates the multilayered effects of Concha Méndez's displacement from her homeland and the cultural milieu of Madrid. Describing her experiences in the Spanish capital during a period of changing social perceptions of gender, Méndez narrates her attempts to construct her subjectivity as a female writer and intellectual in a male-dominated cultural sphere. Engaging in the representation of city life and cultural practices in a collaborative memory text that raises important questions relating to genre and authorial presence, Méndez seeks to revise Spanish literary history and to inscribe herself into the literary record of her country. Placing herself at the center of the canonical "Generation of 1927," Méndez speaks out in her oral testimony to emphasize her integration in this group, her important cultural contributions, and her acceptance by her male contemporaries. Simultaneously, the

Méndez-Ulacia text highlights the difficulties faced by women when attempting to establish themselves in the ambivalent cultural environment of Madrid of the 1920s and early 1930s, as she reveals the processes of exclusion designed to deny women agency on the cultural scene.

Conclusion: Revising Literary History: Memory, Writing, and Identity

THE LIFE-WRITING PRODUCED BY CARMEN BAROJA, MARÍA MARTÍNEZ SIerra, María Teresa León, and Concha Méndez offers important insights into the situation of women who sought to participate in the literary and cultural arena in Spain in the first decades of the twentieth century. Despite the obvious differences among these four writers, in terms of such factors as age, family support for their creative pursuits, and the levels of their political involvement, important parallels may nevertheless be drawn between them, as this study has demonstrated. Raised and educated in a similar fashion, these women were all based in Madrid and were writing during a time of significant cultural and political developments. They were thus all influenced by the intellectual and social climate of the day, and their life-writing reveals some common concerns and attitudes. Furthermore, that these writers all had ties to prominent literary figures of the period is central to an understanding of their positioning in the literary world. Studied together, the autobiographical narratives of Baroja, Martínez Sierra, León, and Méndez reveal the diverse ways in which these writers negotiated their complex positioning in the male-dominated cultural domain and indicate their varied responses to the processes of social change that were taking place during this period.

The question of the class positioning of the women who form the basis of this study is significant. As cultured, middle-class women, the mark of economic privilege clearly characterises their life stories, giving them opportunities not available to their working-class contemporaries. Given the widespread illiteracy among women at this time and their strict social roles, proletarian women were highly unlikely to write or participate in the cultural arena, having neither the time nor the preparation to do so. However, the reality of their class identity also contributed to the restrictions that these writers faced, with the prevailing gender discourse premised on the ideal of the *ángel del hogar* advocating a life dedicated exclusively to the domestic for bourgeois women. The constraints that this ideology imposed on women with cultural interests are evidenced particularly in Baroja's account, in which she expresses her frustration and resentment at the domestic life prescribed for her by the gendered norms of social conduct. Méndez also points to the way in which the social norms of the time limited women's freedom of movement, noting that they needed chaperones to go out in public and were restricted to moving in certain parts of the city.

While the economic resources of their families meant that the four writers studied did receive a certain level of education, this tended to be of a highly conservative nature, with education policies of the time drawing on dominant gender discourse. In addition, women generally attended school only up until their early teenage years, and their education certainly did not extend to tertiary study. The exception in this regard is Martínez Sierra, who received a liberal education with the full support of her parents and went on to train to be a teacher. In contrast, Méndez laments the fact that she was denied access to education past the age of fourteen and was not permitted to read at home. The perceived pernicious effects of reading and study are also noted in the accounts of both Baroja and León, although León nevertheless had access to "forbidden" texts and alternative models and ideas in her relatives' homes.

In general, these women received little family support for their cultural endeavors, again with the exception of Martínez Sierra and, to some extent, León. Baroja's situation was unquestionably the most difficult in this regard, as her account highlights her mother's disapproval of her daughter's interests outside the home and the strict gender roles that prevailed in her household, impeding her participation in the public cultural sphere. While the prominence of Baroja's brothers did give her some access to the cultural arena of turn-of-the-century Madrid, she nevertheless criticizes their lack of support for her endeavors, and argues that, despite their views to the contrary, she was their intellectual equal, or would have been had she had the same educational opportunities that they enjoyed. Moreover, after her marriage, the situation for Baroja certainly did not improve, as her husband was unsupportive of her artistic and intellectual pursuits and, in fact, further hindered her participation in the cultural world. This aspect of Baroja's past differentiates her life story from those of Martínez Sierra, León, and Méndez, all of whom arguably gained greater access to the masculinist intellectual domain as a result of their marriages.

This is certainly the case for Méndez. While, like Baroja, she also faced strong disapproval from her parents of her literary activities and was restricted by the rigidity of her bourgeois environment, following her marriage to Altolaguirre she was integrated into a far more stimulating environment, sharing with her husband common cultural interests and networks. Likewise, the marriages of María Martínez Sierra to Gregorio and of León to Alberti were very important in terms of their access to and integration in the intellectual scene of the day, providing them with valuable opportunities to participate in literary discussions, publish in many of the same outlets as their male peers, and engage with other writers and intellectuals of the day.

Significantly, these three writers all praise their husbands' literary talents in their life-writing, and in some cases position themselves as distinctly secondary to them. While not portraying her literary talents as inferior to those of her husband as explicitly as do Martínez Sierra and León, Méndez nevertheless pays tribute to Altolaguirre's literary talent and cultural contributions in her memoirs, despite their separation. Likewise, Martínez Sierra expresses admiration for Gregorio's work, and the fact that she chose to maintain the myth of collaboration, silencing her own role in their literary production, served to enhance and protect Gregorio's reputation, even after he left her for another woman. León is similarly appreciative of Alberti's talents, with her description of herself as the "tail of the comet" indicating his prominence. However, the admiration that León expresses for Alberti is perhaps more understandable, given that she enjoyed with her husband an enduring marriage and rich creative partnership that lasted until her death in 1988.

Literary history has replicated the subordination of these writers to their husbands. Gregorio Martínez Sierra, Rafael Alberti, and Manuel Altolaguirre have all been incorporated into canonical records of the period to a far greater extent than have their wives or their other female contemporaries. The exclusionary politics of literary history and the concomitant marginalisation of women writers of this era has resulted in their works having received very little critical attention until recent years. In addition, the principal literary movements of early twentieth-century Spain, such as Modernism, were cultural practices that privileged a male subject position, a bias that is further enshrined in generational theory. Although the generational model that has dominated traditional Spanish literary history has been rejected by critics as narrow and elitist, it nevertheless continues to constitute the principal means of referring to the writers and movements of this period, with the "Generation of 1898" and the "Generation of 1927" dominating discussions of literary production of the early twentieth century. That no women are generally included in these groupings, despite the fact that women such as those included in this study did participate in the literary and cultural developments of the time, signals the way in which this hegemonic vision of literary history privileges certain texts and authors, rendering others invisible. Moreover, the masculinist nature of the dominant literary models of this period raises the question of the extent to which Baroja, Martínez Sierra, León, and Méndez engaged with or refused such discourses, and the way in which they portray their positioning in relation to the literary center in their life-writing.

While Baroja does represent the gendering of the public/private spatial division to some extent in her account, noting that certain sites of intellectual activity were closed to her as a woman, this author does not comment specifically on the trends and movements that dominated the cultural panorama in the first decades of the twentieth century. Nevertheless, she expresses an affinity with the writers deemed to belong to the "Generation of 1898," associating her own attitudes and preoccupations with those that dominated the writings of central members of this group. However, Baroja does not argue in *Recuerdos* that she should be considered to have been an integral member of this "generation," despite the fact that the title of her memoirs suggests precisely such a stance.

Méndez, in contrast, insists in *Memorias* on her central role in the "Generation of 1927," expressing resentment at her exclusion from formulations of the canonical "generation" and seeking to inscribe herself into a literary history that has silenced her participation in the activities of this group. This is, in fact, the principal motivation for Méndez's decision to record her memories of her past. Méndez does not, however, explicitly refer to herself or her literary works as "Modernist" in her account, in spite of her association with the "generation" and her involvement in the publication of important Modernist journals of the period. Rather, Méndez firmly positions herself as a *moderna,* depicting herself as the prototype of the "new woman" by highlighting the ways in which she embraced the modern developments of the time, contrary to the social norms that sought to limit her participation in urban life.

Martínez Sierra's relationship to Modernism is similarly complex. This writer explicitly rejects claims that the activities and literary works in which she "collaborated" with Gregorio should be considered to belong to this movement, despite critics concurring that she and her husband were, in fact, central figures in the development of Modernist culture in Madrid. Significantly, the literary journal *Helios* which the Martínez Sierras published, in collaboration with three other writers, was considered to be one of the most important Modernist publications of the period.

In the case of León, neither the dominant literary movements of the 1920s and 1930s nor her own identity as a writer within such groups are central to her reflections in *Memoria*. Rather, as discussed, León focuses on her political and cultural activities, despite the fact that her autobiography reveals her participation in the literary circles of the Spanish capital. Moreover, contemporary critics argue for her inclusion in discussions of the "Generation of 1927," indicating the way in which León's early publications reflect the avant-garde poetics of the time. However, this author, in contrast to Méndez, does not express resentment at her marginalisation from literary history nor does she discuss the exclusionary politics of the cultural world, pointing to quite different motivations for her autobiographical project.

Also of significance is the way in which these writers represent their positioning in relation to one another and to their other female contemporaries. There was almost certainly some contact among the four women who form the basis of this study, given that they were all members of the Madrid branch of the Lyceum Club and they moved in similar social and literary circles. Furthermore, they had connections to some of the same male literary figures of the day: Alberti, for example, who served as Mendez's principal mentor in the early stages of her career, later married León. However, the writers studied do not foreground any such connections between them in their life-writing, nor do they point to the existence of a community of female intellectuals in Madrid in more general terms, with the possible exception of references to the Lyceum Club.

In part, the fact that their accounts do not depict their participation in such a network simply indicates that it did not exist; this is, for example, the case for Baroja, whose memoirs portray her intense isolation, apart from her limited contact with other women with similar interests through the Mirlo Blanco and the Lyceum. Méndez, however, was without doubt in contact with a number of her female contemporaries, some of whom published their works in the literary journals edited by Méndez and Altolaguirre and who attended the regular gatherings held in their home. That Méndez chooses to silence these connections is associated with her insistence throughout her memoirs on both her exceptionality as a female pioneer and her integration in the male-dominated literary world, in which she presents herself as participating alongside her male peers. Likewise, in *Gregorio y yo,* Martínez Sierra depicts herself as collaborating on equal terms with her male contemporaries. This writer does not focus on the limitations imposed on women in the literary sphere nor does she present herself as part of a community of women writers, thus downplaying the exclusionary nature of the literary arena. It is only in her descriptions of her activities in the political sphere in *Una mujer* that she makes reference to some collaboration with other women. For León, it is likewise in relation to her nonliterary endeavors that she foregrounds the question of the position of women in society. While she does make reference to some of her female contemporaries in the literary arena, she also notes the general isolation in which they worked and the lack of a strong community of women writers.

As noted above, the one cultural affiliation that Baroja, Martínez Sierra, León, and Méndez did have in common was their involvement in the Lyceum Club in the late 1920s and early 1930s. Moreover, all four women discuss this organization in their life-writing, albeit from quite distinct perspectives. That the most positive portrayal of the Lyceum Club is that written by Baroja is perhaps unsurprising, given the dearth of other opportunities for her to be involved in the cultural arena. In the case of León, it is the progressive nature of the Club and its objective to work for the advancement of women that she emphasizes in her account, although the Lyceum was perhaps not as essential for her efforts to establish her identity in the cultural world as it was for Baroja. Méndez, too, signals the value of the Lyceum Club in providing a physical space for women to meet and organize their own *tertulias,* although she does simultaneously express an awareness of the limitations of this organization. Likewise, Martínez Sierra acknowledges the restricted influence of the Lyceum Club, noting the fact that it catered only for a small number of women from the middle and upper classes and was certainly not an overtly feminist organization.

The Lyceum Club was not immune to the social and political changes that took place in the early 1930s, a period in which Spanish daily life became overtaken with politics, and, as in other parts of Europe, politics were frequently imbricated with aesthetics. As a result, Baroja argues, the Lyceum Club became too dominated by political discussions at this time, an opinion that is in direct contrast with the views expressed by Martínez Sierra and Méndez, both of whom depict the Lyceum as too conservative and bourgeois to be effective. Thus the division that became apparent between the older and younger members of the Lyceum Club that Méndez signals in her memoirs with her reference to some of the members as *maridas* is reflected in the different attitudes of the women included in this study, with Baroja representative of the older, more conservative members of the Club.

Despite the criticisms of the Lyceum Club made by some of its members, as well as condemnation of its activities from other sectors of society, this organization nevertheless represented an important center of intellectual activity for women in a period in which very few such opportunities existed. On balance, it is presented by all four writers studied here as an institution that was important for women who had no other outlet for their artistic and intellectual talents in 1920s and 1930s Madrid. In 1939, at the end of the Civil War, the Lyceum Club was closed and its records were destroyed. The building that had housed the Club was appropriated by the Falange, and became the Medina Club of the Sección Femenina.

The distinct attitudes towards the Lyceum Club expressed by Baroja, Martínez Sierra, León, and Méndez reflect, to a great extent, their differing levels of interest and involvement in the political sphere. All four of the writers discussed lived through a war that proved to be a politically defining moment for their country, and the consequences of this event inevitably shaped their life stories and thus their narrative accounts of the past. Baroja was the only one of these women who was not a supporter of the Republic and was not politically active in any way. She criticizes actions taken by those on both the left and the right during the 1930s in *Recuerdos* and, overall, her position is the most conservative of the women studied, due largely to her education and family environment. While the levels of political involvement of the other women studied vary, all three clearly express their support for the Republican cause and, as a result of the outcome of the war, spent the postwar years in exile in other European countries and in the Americas. Only Baroja's narrative offers the perspective of a woman who experienced the immediate postwar period in Spain. However, her memoirs were written in the early 1940s, so it is only the first years of this period of Spanish history that she depicts, with her proximity to the events that she describes inevitably affecting her account.

Likewise, Martínez Sierra wrote her autobiographical works in the 1930s and 1940s, during and soon after the turbulent events in Spain that led to her exile. Martínez Sierra's visibility as a female political figure who adopted a formal parliamentary role during the Republican period sets her apart from her contemporaries, and gives this writer a greater understanding of the complex discourses of gender and class that prevailed in her sociohistorical context. It also makes her chosen anonymity in the literary world all the more striking. While Martínez Sierra spent the postwar years in exile in France and, later, in the Americas, the representation of her experiences as exiled subject is not central to either of her accounts.

In contrast, both León and Méndez reflect on their experiences of exile in their life-writing, in works that were written and recorded in the 1960s and 1980s respectively. In *Memorias habladas,* Méndez highlights her isolation during this period in which she was displaced from her homeland and from the literary center, an isolation made all the more intense by her separation from her husband. While she does not reflect at length on the political situation in Spain, neither in terms of the events of the 1930s nor with regard to the years of the Franco regime, Méndez's account nevertheless clearly reveals her support for the Republic and her involvement in the public sphere during the war years, despite the fact that she was not affiliated to any specific political party.

In contrast, León expresses a firm commitment to the principles of the Communist Party, and she was at the forefront of many of the cultural activities that took place in the Republican zone during the war. Her political activism and public speaking roles mean that she had much in common with Martínez Sierra. Both women represented left-wing political parties and sought specifically to denounce injustices that affected the working classes and women, although Martínez Sierra undoubtedly adopted a more overtly feminist stance in *Una mujer* and in her speeches and other writings than did León in her works. However, the forms of feminism espoused by both Martínez Sierra and León reflect their political positioning, with the class structure seen by both women as the primary obstacle to women's emancipation.

In the case of León, exile and its effects constitute the focus of much of her autobiographical narrative, as she highlights the cultural production of her generation and the way in which the outcome of the Civil War cut short the literary and social developments of the 1920s and 1930s. In particular, León highlights the need for the voices of exiled Spaniards to be heard in their homeland, urging her compatriots not to allow the collective memory of Spain's recent historical past to be lost. For writers and intellectuals such as León, then, the Republican years became a nostalgic memory following the Nationalist victory in the Civil War in 1939. As such, the memory process is presented as a particularly important tool for reconstituting the exiled self, with the act of remembering the past linked to the formulation of an identity in the present.

The different approaches to memory adopted in the life-writing of Baroja, Martínez Sierra, León, and Méndez reveal the complexities of the process of remembering. Their narratives demonstrate that remembering the past self involves a continuous process of partial reconstruction, rather than the restoration of an original "true" identity. While all four writers acknowledge, to some degree, the provisionality and incompleteness of memories of the past and question the kind and degree of "truth" that can be expected from autobiographical writing, only León theorizes about the workings of memory in her narrative. This writer both explores her own memories of past and self and analyses the very nature of the process of remembering in her work, reflecting on the functioning of memory on both a personal and collective level and, most importantly, emphasizing the need for the events of the past to be rearticulated and remembered.

In 1939, as a result of the Republican defeat in the Spanish Civil War, literary and social modernism came to an abrupt end in Spain, and the progress that had been achieved in terms of women's roles in society was dramatically reversed by the Franco regime. The literary accomplishments and cultural contributions of Baroja, Martínez Sierra, León, and Méndez, as well as those of many of their contemporaries, were excluded from the historical record of their country and have only recently begun to be reincorporated into the annals of cultural and literary history. The life-writing produced by these four writers casts new light on the positioning of the female intellectual in 1920s and 1930s Madrid, in terms of their varied negotiations with aspects of their environment, the gender politics of their era, and the discourses of the "modern" that prevailed in 1920s and 1930s Madrid.

Notes

INTRODUCTION

1. The four writers studied in this book will be referred to by their surnames throughout; thus all references to "Baroja" are to Carmen Baroja and all references to "Martínez Sierra" are to María Martínez Sierra, and so on, unless otherwise specified.

2. Unless otherwise indicated, the translations of all Spanish citations in this book are my own. Due to restrictions of space, I give the original quotations in Spanish in addition to the English translations, only for material from works by Baroja, Martínez Sierra, León, and Méndez.

3. To indicate that this study seeks to question the validity of the generational model, references to these groups will be placed in quotation marks when used in this book (hence, "Generation of 1927").

4. In contrast, Mary-Lee Bretz suggests that there was not, in fact, a notable increase in the number of women writers during this period, but she does note their heightened visibility in the public cultural arena (2001, 418).

5. This list is not exhaustive; for further details see Cristina Ruiz Guerrero (1997, 156).

6. In this study, I have chosen to refer to this writer as María Martínez Sierra, the name under which she published her life-writing, rather than as María Lejárraga.

7. Baroja also published a number of articles in journals and magazines, as well as two museum collection catalogues in the late 1940s. Other writings by Baroja remain unpublished.

8. Also of relevance regarding this period of Spanish literary history is Roberta Johnson's study of gender and nation in the Modernist novel and Mary-Lee Bretz's recent work on Spanish Modernism. See Johnson (2003) and Bretz (2001).

9. Relevant studies include those by Timothy Dow Adams (1990), Paul John Eakin (1992, 1999), Paul Jay (1984), James Olney (1998), and Paul Smith (1988). For work dealing specifically with women's life-writing, see the essays collected in the studies by Shari Benstock (1988), Estelle Jelinek (1980b), and Domna Stanton (1987). See also Sidonie Smith (1987).

10. See Caballé (1995), Fernández (1992), and Louriero (1991).

CHAPTER 1. THE WOMAN WRITER

1. See, for example, Dámaso Alonso (1952), F. J. Díez de Revenga (1987), Vicente Gaos (1965), and Ángel González (1976).

2. Mainer makes only brief mention of León, as co-founder of the publication *Octubre* and in a list of contributors to a 1936 publication (1983, 320–21).

3. The question of generations was also discussed in Spain by José Ortega y Gasset and his followers, most notably Julián Marías (1949). However, Ortega's notion of the generation, literary or otherwise, is less narrow than conceptions based more closely on the German model which have come to dominate literary criticism. For further discussion of this question, see Christopher Soufas (1989, 15–17).

4. Critics of the generational model include John Butt (1980), Ricardo Gullón (1969), Soufas (1989, 1991–92), and Michael Ugarte (1994). It should be noted that the "Generation of 1927" label was also disclaimed by some of the group's purported members. See Fajardo and Wilcox (1983, 13–14).

5. See also Javier Blasco for a discussion of the "Generation of 1898," which, he argues, "was nothing more than an artificial construction by historians" (2000, 121).

6. This is true of the process of canon formation and the classification of literary works by genre in more general terms; as Robert Elbaz has noted, "[g]eneric classification is a hegemonic phenomenon which restricts literary practice to approved, institutionalized forms of expression" (1988, 14–15). The generational model is, however, more restrictive, in that it is extremely rigid and narrow, deeming only a very small number of writers and works to be worthy of inclusion. For further discussion of the issue of canon formation more generally, see the essays collected in Robert von Hallberg's *Canons* (1984), particularly Barbara Herrnstein Smith's "Contingencies of Value" (1984).

7. For a discussion of the terms "modernization," "modernism," and "modernity," see Rita Felski (1995, 12–13). Malcolm Bradbury and James McFarlane (1991), among others, set the temporal parameters of Modernism at 1890 to 1930, although Ricardo Quinones (1985) extends the period to 1940. Other useful texts on Modernism include those by Peter Brooker (1992), Astradur Eysteinsson (1990), Anthony Geist and José Monleón (1999), and Ricardo Gullón (1990).

8. It is important to note the traditional difference in usage between the broader English term "Modernism" and the more limited use of the term *"modernismo"* in Spanish, which referred to the movement that originated in Latin America with the work of Rubén Darío, among others. See Bretz (2001, 23–27) for a discussion of this distinction.

9. See Bretz (2001, 36–38). See also Ramos (1989) for further discussion of Latin American Modernism.

10. See Kirkpatrick (1999). See also Tyrus Miller (1999) for a discussion of late Modernism.

11. For further detail, see Inman Fox (1997) and Bretz (2001, 61–63). The term "Generation of 1898" was, however, in use earlier. Following initial references to such a group made by Azorín (José Martínez Ruiz) in 1905 and 1907, his two articles published in the newspaper *ABC* in 1913 led to the development of the concept of the "Generation of 1898."

12. Relevant texts are Salinas's "El problema del modernismo en España o un conflicto entre dos espíritus" and "El concepto de generación literaria aplicada a la del 98" in Salinas (1941). See also Laín Entralgo (1945, 1970) and Guillermo Díaz-Plaja (1951).

13. Conversely, Quinones has described Modernism as an aesthetic that is "more in search of the virile hard line" (1985, 55).

14. For a discussion of the avant-garde movement in Spain, see Derek Harris (1995). The male-dominated nature of such movements is replicated in Harris's text, in which none of the essays focuses on women involved in the avant-garde cultural scene.

15. For detailed information on this historical period, see José Álvarez Junco and Adrian Shubert (2000), Charles Esdaile (2000), José María Jover Zamora, Guadalupe Gómez-Ferrer Morant and Juan Pablo Fusi Aizpúrua (2001), and Gabriel Tortella (2000).

16. It is important to recognize that there were differences in levels of and attitudes to women's participation in the workforce in different regions of Spain and in urban versus rural areas, affecting women's experiences. For detailed statistical information on the situation in Madrid, which is the focus of this study, see Pilar Folguera (1995).

17. For a detailed discussion of Marañón's theories, see Mary Nash (1999).

18. Spain's neutrality in the war is described by Fernando Díaz-Plaja as "a half truth," as he notes that "the state, the government was neutral, but the people, the nation, passionately supported one side or the other of the opposing forces" (1973, 9).

19. For detailed discussions and data regarding women in the workforce in early twentieth-century Spain, see Rosa María Capel Martínez (1986), Nash (1983), and Geraldine Scanlon (1986, 58–121).

20. See also Andrew Debicki (1981, 60) and Salvador Jiménez-Fajardo (1985, 21). Soufas, however, disputes the reading of the poets of the "Generation of 1927" as essentially nonideological (1989, xiv–xv).

21. For a discussion of the intellectual and ideological origins of the Republic, see Enrique Montero (1995).

22. For further discussion of the figure of the "modern woman," see Nancy Cott (1994) and Angelique Richardson and Chris Willis (2001). With regard to the emergence of this model in Spain, see María Gloria Nuñéz Pérez (1993, 29) and Mangini (2001, 74–76).

23. While women were officially granted the right to vote in municipal elections in 1924 during the Primo de Rivera dictatorship (1923–30), no such elections were held. For a detailed discussion of the legal rights of women in Spain between 1868 and 1931, see Scanlon (1986, 122–58).

24. See Scanlon (1986, 265, 308, 274).

25. This is not to say that women did not participate in political action; it simply refers to their absence from formal political institutions. See the essays in Enders and Radcliff (1999) for studies of women's involvement in such political activities as tobacco factory strikes and consumer riots.

26. As Nash has argued, this reflects a broader trend in Spanish political culture, which tended not to focus on the importance of political rights. See Nash (1999, 30–31).

27. See Leggott (2001) for discussion of Ibárruri's political role and her autobiographical writings.

28. See Scanlon (1986, 15–57) for details of women's education in Spain in the period from 1868 to 1931, including a discussion of the significance of the progressive ideals of the *krausistas* [Krausists] and the *Institución Libre de Enseñanza* [Institute of Independent Education]. See also Carolyn Boyd (1997, 3–64).

29. See Consuelo Flecha García (1996) for a detailed discussion of the situation for women in the sphere of higher education.

30. This study focuses on the cultural scene in the capital, Madrid; thus the parallel developments that were taking place in Barcelona in the Catalan context are not discussed here. For relevant information, see Guillermo Díaz-Plaja (1975, 137–41) and Temma Kaplan (1992).

31. Zulueta and Moreno's text (1993) provides a comprehensive study of the history and functions of the *Residencia de Señoritas*. See also John Crispin (1981, 59–64).

32. Benavente's refusal to speak at the Lyceum Club is noted by Mangini (2001, 91), as well as in the memoirs of Baroja (1998), León (1998), and Méndez (1990). It should also be noted that Alberti's position with regard to the Lyceum has been seen as ambiguous, with the lecture that he presented in November 1929 dressed as a clown causing some debate. See Mangini (2001, 91–92).

33. Interestingly, this model is also found in Freud's writings. See Nicola King (2000, 12–20) for a detailed discussion of these contrasting approaches to memory.

34. For detailed discussions of the question of factual accuracy and truthtelling in life-writing, see Eakin (2004).

35. See Shoshana Felman and Dori Laub (1992), Geoffrey Hartman (1994), Berel Lang (1999), and James Young (1988, 1993).

36. See Benstock (1988), Tess Cosslett, Celia Lury, and Penny Summerfield (2000), Jelinek (1980b), Laura Marcus (1994), Sidonie Smith (1987), and Stanton (1987).

37. Critics such as Benstock (1988) adopt the term "life-writing" in order to avoid the limitations of the traditional category of "autobiography" and to include a wide range of writings such as diaries, journals, memoirs, and autobiographical fiction.

38. For work on life-writing by Spanish women, see Caballé (1998), Leggott (2001), Mangini (1995), Lydia Masanet (1998), and Bettina Pacheco (2001).

Chapter 2. Carmen Baroja y Nessi

1. Baroja's two children who survived into adulthood, Julio Caro Baroja and Pío Caro Baroja, were born in 1914 and 1928 respectively.

2. Note, however, that Juan Ramón Jiménez was only seventeen in 1898, yet he has been identified with the "Generation of 1898."

3. Unlike Baroja, Méndez does insist on her role as an integral member of a canonical literary generation, in her case, the "Generation of 1927," as will be discussed in chapter 5.

4. While both Martín Gaite and Mangini are referring to the immediate post–Civil War period in Spain, the prevailing ideology regarding women was remarkably similar to that which is pertinent to Baroja.

5. María Goyri was María Teresa León's aunt, and was also an important model for León, as will be discussed in chapter 4.

6. Baroja's views here with regard to the Lyceum Club contrast with those expressed by Martínez Sierra and Méndez, both of whom depict the Lyceum as conservative and bourgeois, as will be discussed in chapters 3 and 5.

7. Baroja's views on the changes in the Lyceum Club are also documented by her son, Julio Caro Baroja (1992, 64–65).

8. See Graham (1995a) for a discussion of the social history of women in 1940s Spain.

9. *Ateneos* were meeting houses for those associated with the anarchist movement.

10. Pío Baroja was, however, by no means a Monarchist, as Julio Caro Baroja notes (1992, 79).

11. For detailed discussion of life in the Nationalist zone during the years of the Civil War, see Rafael Abella (1973).

12. Graham also makes reference to the "savage poverty" that characterized these years (1995a, 183).

13. Hurtado confirms that there are indeed both distortions and omissions in Baroja's text, relating to details such as the author's age and her literary publications (1998b, 14).

Chapter 3. María Martínez Sierra

1. These stories have recently been republished in Isabel Lizarraga Vizcarra's *María Lejárraga, Pedagoga* (2004).

2. The question of the "collaboration" between Martínez Sierra and her husband is discussed later in this chapter. In this study, I follow Alda Blanco (1989, 2000) in placing quotation marks around the name "Gregorio Martínez Sierra" to refer to the author of works written by María but published under Gregorio's name.

3. Bretz (2001, 34) also notes that *Renacimiento* dedicated considerable space within its pages to Catalan writers.

4. These volumes are entitled *Cartas a las mujeres de España* [Letters to the Women of Spain] (1916), *Feminismo, feminidad, españolismo* [Feminism, Femininity, Spanishness] (1917), *La mujer moderna* [The Modern Woman] (1920), and *Nuevas cartas a las mujeres de España* [New Letters to the Women of Spain] (1932). For detailed discussion of these essays, see Blanco (1998).

5. This quotation comes from the essay "De feminismo" [On Feminism], which appeared in the volume *Feminismo, feminidad, españolismo* (1917) and is the text of a lecture presented by Gregorio Martínez Sierra in the Eslava Theatre in 1917.

6. This was the name given to the organization previously known as the Comité Nacional de las Mujeres Contra la Guerra y el Fascismo [National Committee of Women Against War and Fascism], and later as Mujeres Antifascistas [Antifascist Women], after the organization was declared illegal following the Asturian revolution. See Scanlon (1986, 297–99) for further information.

7. For discussion of "Gregorio Martínez Sierra's" feminist theories, see Scanlon (1986, 197–98, 289–90).

8. For extensive discussion and documentation of the "collaborative" relationship between María and Gregorio Martínez Sierra, as well as detailed biographical information, see Patricia O'Connor (1977, 2003) and Antonina Rodrigo (1994). For discussions of other aspects of Martínez Sierra's work, see Juan Aguilera Sastre (2002) and Blanco (1989, 1998, 2000, 2003).

9. For further information on Gregorio Martínez Sierra, see Ana María Arias de Cossío (1991) and Augusto Martínez Olmedilla (1947, 217–55; 1961, 247–49).

10. Martínez Sierra's insistence that their works be considered realist may also be linked to the author's sociopolitical commitment.

11. There is a political element also to León's *Memoria de la melancolía,* as will be discussed in chapter 4, but her work is, on balance, less propagandistic than is Martínez Sierra's *Una mujer.*

12. The factionalization of political forces on the left during the Spanish Civil War has been well documented by historians. See, for example, Raymond Carr (2000), Esdaile (2000), and Paul Preston (1986).

13. In this respect, Martínez Sierra's account is also reminiscent of Constancia de la Mora's *In Place of Splendor* (1939).

14. The Casas del Pueblo were the socialist movement's workers' meeting houses, which were centers for political activity, education, and relaxation.

15. The question of women's relationship to the urban environment will be explored in chapter 5 with regard to Méndez.

16. Despite this theoretical commitment to sexual equality, the notion that women and men were equals caused much debate within socialist ranks. It should also be noted that two key figures in the Socialist Party, Indalecio Prieto and Julián Besteiro, left the debating chamber when the vote on women's suffrage was taken to indicate their opposition to this legislation. For a detailed discussion on women and socialism in Spain, see Nash (1981, 137–73).

17. Similar interpretations of the consequences of granting women the vote are expressed by Capel Martínez (1975, 245–46, 255, 271), Gerald Brenan (1950, 266), and Manuel Tuñón de Lara (1976, 12).

18. As was noted in chapter 1, the women's groups that emerged in Spain in the first decades of the twentieth century were generally conservative, middle-class organizations. This was true of the groups in which Martínez Sierra participated, such as the Asociación Femenina de Educación Cívica and the Lyceum Club.

CHAPTER 4. MARÍA TERESA LEÓN

1. León's use of the third-person voice in parts of her account will be discussed later in this chapter.

2. The lack of family support experienced by Méndez will be discussed in chapter 5.

3. The way in which a woman's identity is considered to depend on her association with a man is highlighted by the following reference to Goyri which appears in a 1997 article on León's work by Salvador Oropesa: "For those who may not remember, Goyri was the wife of don Ramón Menéndez Pidal, she was the one who wrote ballads on their honeymoon" (1997, 130).

4. For detailed discussion of León's different literary works, see Juan Carlos Estébanez Gil (1995) and Gregorio Torres Nebrera (1987, 1996).

5. León published a booklet entitled *La historia tiene la palabra* (1944) that defended the committee's project to safeguard the artistic patrimony of their country, in response to criticism from experts in the field who had questioned their suitability for undertaking such a task.

6. Among these more recent works is a special issue of the journal *Letras Peninsulares* (Vásquez 2004) dedicated primarily to studies of León's works and *Memoria de la hermosura* (2005), edited by Olga Álvarez de Armas. See also Neira (2004).

7. Examples of such narratives include the autobiographies of Formica (1982, 1984, 1998), Ibárruri (1984, 1992), Pilar Jaraiz Franco (1981), and Federica Montseny (1987). See Leggott (2001) and Mangini (1995) for further discussion of these works and of this characteristic in autobiographies of the period.

8. León makes reference in *Memoria* to the extraordinary role played by Ibárruri in the Republican war effort and to the dichotomous representations of the Communist leader. She also recalls that the two women both spoke at a political rally in Asturias in 1936 and that she saw Ibárruri in the postwar years in Moscow (1998, 245–46).

9. See Estébanez Gil (1995, 57–58) for a listing of the numerous people to whom León refers in *Memoria*.

10. The autobiographical nature of *Juego limpio* (1987) is similarly noted by other critics, among them Torres Nebrera, who affirms that "lo testimonial y autobiográfico alcanza su mayor y mejor registro literario" [the testimonial and autobiographical achieve their highest and best literary register] in this novel (1998, 26).

11. See the recent article by Helena López (2004) for further discussion of *Memoria* in relation to feminist discourse.

12. For a discussion of the development and uses of the categories of "high" and "low" culture in the Spanish context, see Stephanie Sieburth (1994). Sieburth also argues that this discourse is closely linked to the desire to keep gender roles distinct.

13. Among those mentioned is Martínez Sierra (León 1998, 513).

14. The negative reaction of their peers to their activism on behalf of the Spanish Communist Party is confirmed in Méndez's memoirs, in which she is critical of Alberti and his communist affiliation, as will be seen in chapter 5.

15. See Nash (1995) for detailed discussion of women's involvement in the Spanish Civil War.

16. In a recent article dealing with León's memories of exile in *Memoria,* Ofelia Ferrán refers to the "disidentification" that León's text manifests and likewise points to "the manner in which the problem of gender is inextricably intertwined with the problem of exile" (2005, 62).

17. This generation gap between exiled Spaniards and the youth of Spain is likewise described by Max Aub in *La gallina ciega* (1995, 243–44).

18. For further discussion of this process, see Joan Ramón Resina (2000).

19. The exhumation of the numerous mass graves from the Civil War is part of this process. For detailed discussion, see Montse Armengou and Ricard Belis (2004) and Emilio Silva and Santiago Macías (2003).

CHAPTER 5. CONCHA MÉNDEZ

1. In addition, a number of plays written by Méndez remain unpublished, and some of her dramatic works were never staged. Méndez also wrote plays for children. It is, however, as a poet that Méndez is better known. For discussion of Mén-

dez's dramatic works, see Emilio Miró (2001), Nieva de la Paz (2001), and James Valender (2001a).

2. The couple's first child, born in 1933, died shortly after birth.

3. For biographical and bibliographical information pertinent to Méndez and Altolaguirre, see Valender (2001b, 2001c).

4. See, for example, Sherna Berger Gluck and Daphne Patai (1991), Selma Leydesdorff, Luisa Passerini, and Paul Thompson (1996), and Paul Thompson (1988).

5. Such attitudes are exposed in texts by writers such as Vicente Aleixandre, Rafael Gómez de la Serna, and Pablo Neruda (reproduced in Valender 2001b), as well as in Carlos Morla Lynch's diary (1958) and in Pedro Salinas's letters (1992).

6. See, for example, Juan Manuel Rozas (1978, 26). Other critics suggest the dates 1891 to 1902; see Debicki (1994, 18).

7. This last claim is inaccurate; Méndez's presentation of the Lyceum Club in her memoirs is discussed later in this chapter.

8. See Dinverno (2003) for an excellent discussion of Méndez's representations of space in *Memorias*.

9. Bellver (2001, 38) similarly notes that the Lyceum became known as the "husbandettes' club," suggesting that this description was in quite common usage at the time. See also Martín Gaite (1992, 19). Méndez's comments that the wives of eminent men simply repeated their husbands' opinions at the Club replicates the representation of the Lyceum that appeared in José Díaz Fernández's 1929 novel, *La venus mecánica* (1989, 105).

10. While the influence of male opinions on the Lyceum Club members may be perceived as negative, it is important to bear in mind that for male voices not to be considered could lead to a form of ghettoization of the culture to emerge from the Lyceum.

11. These roles are also determined by class. Working-class women were not, for example, required to be chaperoned.

12. Buñuel does not mention his relationship with Méndez in his own memoirs, entitled *Mi último suspiro* (1982). For further discussion of the relationship between Méndez and Buñuel, see Ulacia Altolaguirre (1993).

13. See Ruth Fincher and Jane Jacobs (1998), Jo Little, Linda Peake, and Pat Richardson (1988), Daphne Spain (1992), and Elizabeth Wilson (1991).

14. See Quance (2003) for a discussion of Borges's career and of her work as the illustrator of volumes of poetry published by Méndez and Conde.

15. It should, however, be noted that some critics highlight the committed political stance of Latin or Continental European Modernism in contrast with Anglo-American Modernism. See Bradbury and MacFarlane (1991).

Works Cited

Abella, Rafael. 1973. *La vida cotidiana durante la guerra civil: La España nacional.* Barcelona: Planeta.

Adams, Timothy Dow. 1990. *Telling Lies in Modern American Autobiography.* Chapel Hill: University of North Carolina Press.

Aguilar Fernández, Paloma. 2001. *Justicia, política y memoria: Los legados del franquismo en la transición española.* Madrid: Instituto Juan March de Estudios e Investigaciones.

Aguilera Sastre, Juan, ed. 2002. *María Martínez Sierra y la República: Ilusión y compromiso.* Logroño: Instituto de Estudios Riojanos.

Alas, Leopoldo (Clarín). 1897. Revista Literaria, Horizontes: Poesía de Federico Balart. *El Imparcial,* March 15.

Alberti, Rafael. 1987. *La arboleda perdida.* Vol. 2. Barcelona: Seix Barral. (Orig. pub. 1959.)

Alborg, Concha. 1996. *Una mujer por caminos de España:* La seudoautobiografía de María Martínez Sierra (1874–1974). *Revista de Estudios Hispánicos* 30:485–95.

Aldaraca, Bridget A. 1991. *El ángel del hogar: Galdós and the Ideology of Domesticity in Spain.* Chapel Hill: North Carolina Studies in the Romance Languages and Literatures.

Alexander, Gerard. 1999. Women and Men at the Ballot Box: Voting in Spain's Two Democracies. In Enders and Radcliff 1999, 349–74.

Alonso, Dámaso. 1952. *Poetas españoles contemporáneos.* Madrid: Gredos.

Altolaguirre, Maya S. 2003. *María Teresa León: Gran señora de todos los deberes.* Granada: Patronato Federico García Lorca de la Diputación de Granada.

Álvarez, María Antonia. 1989. La autobiografía y sus géneros afines. *Epos: Revista de Filología* 5:439–50.

Álvarez de Armas, Olga, ed. 2005. *María Teresa León: Memoria de la hermosura.* Madrid: Fundación Autor.

Álvarez Junco, José, and Adrian Shubert. 2000. *Spanish History since 1808.* Oxford: Oxford University Press.

Ana, Marcos. 1989. María Teresa León, una mujer comprometida con su tiempo. In *Homenaje a María Teresa León,* 41–50. Madrid: Universidad Complutense de Madrid.

Arias de Cossío, Ana María. 1991. *Dos siglos de escenografía en Madrid.* Madrid: Mondadori.

Arkinstall, Christine R. 2004. *Gender, Class, and Nation: Mercè Rodoreda and the Subjects of Modernism.* Lewisburg, PA: Bucknell University Press.

Armengou, Montse, and Ricard Belis. 2004. *Las fosas del silencio: ¿Hay un holocausto español?* Barcelona: Plaza y Janés.

Aub, Max. 1985. *Conversaciones con Buñuel.* Madrid: Aguilar.

———. 1995. *La gallina ciega: Diario español.* Ed. Manuel Aznar Soler. Barcelona: Alba. (Orig. pub. 1971.)

Baroja, Ricardo. 1952. *Gente de la generación del 98.* Barcelona: Juventud.

Baroja y Nessi, Carmen. 1933. *El encaje en España.* Barcelona: Labor.

———. 1942. *Martinito, el de la Casa Grande.* Barcelona: Juventud.

———. 1945. *Catálogo de la colección de amuletos.* Madrid: Museo del Pueblo Español.

———. 1948–1952. *Catálogo de la colección de pendientes.* 2 vols. Madrid: Museo del Pueblo Español.

———. 1995. *Tres Barojas: Poemas.* Ed. Pío Caro Baroja. Pamplona: Pamiela.

———. 1998. *Recuerdos de una mujer de la generación del 98.* Ed. Amparo Hurtado. Barcelona: Tusquets.

Bellver, Catherine. 1997a. From Illusion to Disappearance: The Fate of the Female Poets of the Generation of 27. *Monographic Review* 13:205–26.

———. 1997b. Literary Influence and Female Creativity: The Case of Two Women Poets of the Generation of 27. *Siglo XX/20th Century* 15:7–31.

———. 2001. *Absence and Presence: Spanish Women Poets of the Twenties and Thirties.* Lewisburg, PA: Bucknell University Press.

Benstock, Shari. 1986. *Women of the Left Bank: Paris, 1900–1940.* Austin: University of Texas Press.

———, ed. 1988. *The Private Self: Theory and Practice of Women's Autobiographical Writings.* London: Routledge.

———. 1989. Expatriate Modernism: Writing on the Cultural Rim. In Broe and Ingram 1989, 19–40.

Beverley, John. 1992. The Margin at the Center: On *Testimonio* (Testimonial Narrative). In Smith and Watson 1992, 91–114.

Bieder, Maryellen. 1992. Woman and the Twentieth-Century Spanish Literary Canon: The Lady Vanishes. *Anales de la Literatura Española Contemporánea* 17:301–24.

Billson, Marcus, and Sidonie Smith. 1980. Lillian Hellman and the Strategy of the "Other." In Jelinek 1980, 163–79.

Blanco, Alda. 1989. Introduction to María Martínez Sierra 1989, 7–40.

———. 1998. A las mujeres de España: The Feminist Essays of María Martínez Sierra. In *Spanish Women Writers and the Essay: Gender, Politics, and the Self,* ed. Kathleen M. Glenn and Mercedes Mazquiarán de Rodríguez, 75–99. Columbia: University of Missouri Press.

———. 2000. Prologue to María Martínez Sierra 2000, 11–42.

———. 2003. *A las mujeres: Ensayos feministas de María Martínez Sierra.* Logroño: Instituto de Estudios Riojanos.

Blasco, Javier. 2000. El "98" que nunca existió. In *Spain's 1898 Crisis: Regenerationism, Modernism, Post-Colonialism,* ed. Joseph Harrison and Alan Hoyle, 121–31. Manchester: Manchester University Press.

Bordons, Teresa. 1993. *Género sexual, literatura e historia: España de finales de siglo a la II República*. PhD diss., University of California San Diego.

Boyd, Carolyn P. 1997. *Historia Patria: Politics, History, and National Identity in Spain, 1875–1975*. Princeton, NJ: Princeton University Press.

Bradbury, Malcolm, and James MacFarlane, eds. 1991. *Modernism: A Guide to European Literature, 1890–1930*. London: Penguin.

Brenan, Gerald. 1950. *The Spanish Labyrinth*. 2nd ed. Cambridge: Cambridge University Press.

Bretz, Mary Lee. 2001. *Encounters Across Borders: The Changing Visions of Spanish Modernism, 1890–1930*. Lewisburg, PA: Bucknell University Press.

Broe, Mary Lynn, and Angela Ingram, eds. 1989. *Women's Writing in Exile*. Chapel Hill: University of North Carolina Press.

Brooker, Peter, ed. 1992. *Modernism/Postmodernism*. London: Longman.

Bruss, Elizabeth W. 1976. *Autobiographical Acts: The Changing Situation of a Literary Genre*. Baltimore: Johns Hopkins University Press.

Buñuel, Luis. 1982. *Mi último suspiro: Memorias*. Trans. Ana María de la Fuente. Mexico City: Plaza y Janés.

Butt, John. 1980. The "Generation of 1898": A Critical Fallacy? *Forum for Modern Language Studies* 16:136–53.

Caballé, Anna. 1995. *Narcisos de tinta: Ensayos sobre la literatura autobiográfica en lengua castellana, siglos XIX y XX*. Málaga: Megazul.

———. 1998. Memorias y autobiografías escritas por mujeres (siglos XIX y XX). In Zavala 1998, 111–37.

Campbell, Karlyn Kohrs. 1989. *Man Cannot Speak for Her: A Critical Study of Early Feminist Rhetoric*. New York: Greenwood.

Capel Martínez, Rosa María. 1975. *El sufragio femenino en la Segunda República*. Granada: Universidad de Granada.

———. 1986. *El trabajo y la educación de la mujer en España (1900–1930)*. Madrid: Ministerio de Cultura, Instituto de la Mujer.

Cardwell, Richard A. 2004. The Poetry of *Modernismo* in Spain. In Gies 2004, 500–12.

Caro Baroja, Julio. 1992. *Los Baroja: Memorias Familiares*. 2nd ed. Madrid: Taurus.

Caro Baroja, Pío. 1996. *Itinerario sentimental: Guía de Itzea*. Pamplona: Pamiela.

Carr, Raymond. 2000. *The Spanish Tragedy: The Civil War in Perspective*. London: Phoenix. (Orig. pub. 1977.)

Caruth, Cathy. 1995. *Unclaimed Experience: Trauma, Narrative, and History*. Baltimore: Johns Hopkins University Press.

Castillo Martín, Marcia. 2001. *Las convidadas de papel: Mujer, memoria y literatura en la España de los años veinte*. Madrid: Ayuntamiento de Alcalá de Henares.

Caudet, Francisco. 1997. *Hipótesis sobre el exilio republicano de 1939*. Madrid: Fundación Universitaria Española.

Chacel, Rosa. 1985. *A la orilla de un pozo*. Valencia: Pre-Textos. (Orig. pub. 1936.)

Checa Puerta, Julio Enrique. 1992. "Los teatros de Gregorio Martínez Sierra." In *El teatro de España: Entre la tradición y la vanguardia, 1918–1939*, ed. Dru Dougherty and María Francisca Vilches de Frutos, 121–26. Madrid: Consejo Superior de Investigaciones Científicas.

Ciplijauskaité, Biruté. 1989. Escribir entre dos exilios: Las voces femeninas de la generación del 27. In *Homenaje al Profesor Antonio Vilanova,* ed. Marta Cristina Carbonell, 2:119–26. Barcelona: Universidad de Barcelona.

Cole, Gregory K. 2000. *Spanish Women Poets of the Generation of 1927.* Lewiston, PA: Mellen.

Comellas, José Luis. 2002. *Del 98 a la semana trágica, 1898–1909: Crisis de conciencia y renovación política.* Madrid: Biblioteca Nueva.

Conde, Carmen. 1967. *Obra poética de Carmen Conde, 1929–1966.* Madrid: Biblioteca Nueva.

Corbett, Mary Jean. 1992. *Representing Femininity: Middle-Class Subjectivity in Victorian and Edwardian Women's Autobiographies.* New York: Oxford University Press.

Cortada, James W., ed. 1982. *Historical Dictionary of the Spanish Civil War, 1936–1939.* Westport, CT: Greenwood Press.

Cosslett, Tess, Celia Lury, and Penny Summerfield, eds. 2000. *Feminism and Autobiography: Texts, Theories, Methods.* London: Routledge.

Cott, Nancy F. 1994. The Modern Woman of the 1920s, American Style. In *A History of Women in the West,* ed. Françoise Thébaud, 5:77–91. Cambridge: Harvard University Press.

Crispin, John. 1981. *Oxford y Cambridge en Madrid: La Residencia de Estudiantes (1910–1936) y su entorno cultural.* Santander: Isla de los Ratones.

Debicki, Andrew P. 1981. *Estudios sobre poesía española contemporánea: La generación de 1924–1925.* Madrid: Gredos.

———. 1994. *Spanish Poetry of the Twentieth Century: Modernity and Beyond.* Lexington: University Press of Kentucky.

Dennis, Nigel. 2004. Prose: Early Twentieth Century. In Gies 2004, 569–78.

Díaz Fernández, José. 1989. *La venus mecánica.* Madrid: Moreno-Avila. (Orig. pub. 1929.)

Díaz-Plaja, Fernando. 1973. *Francófilos y germanófilos: Los españoles en la guerra europea.* Barcelona: Dopesa.

Díaz-Plaja, Guillermo. 1951. *Modernismo frente a Noventa y Ocho: Una introducción a la literatura española del siglo XX.* Madrid: Espasa-Calpe.

———. 1975. *Vanguardismo y protesta en la España de hace medio siglo.* Barcelona: Libros de la Frontera.

Diego, Gerardo. 1962. *Poesía española contemporánea: Antología.* Madrid: Taurus. (Orig. pub. 1934.)

Díez de Revenga, F. J. 1987. *Panorama crítico de la generación del 27.* Madrid: Castalia.

Dinverno, Melissa. 2003. Gendered Geographies: Remapping the Space of the Woman Intellectual in Concha Méndez's *Memorias habladas, memorias armadas. Revista de Estudios Hispánicos* 37:49–74.

Dobón, María Dolores. 1996. *Sociólogos* contra *estetas:* Prehistoria del conflicto entre modernismo y 98. *Hispanic Review* 64:57–72.

Dupláa, Christina. 1996. *La voz testimonial en Montserrat Roig: Estudio cultural de los textos.* Barcelona: Icaria.

———. 2000. *Memoria sí, venganza no en Josefina R. Aldecoa: Ensayo sociohistórico de su narrativa*. Barcelona: Icaria.

Eakin, Paul John. 1992. *Touching the World: Reference in Autobiography*. Princeton, NJ: Princeton University Press.

———. 1999. *How Our Lives Become Stories: Making Selves*. Ithaca: Cornell University Press.

———, ed. 2004. *The Ethics of Life Writing*. Ithaca: Cornell University Press.

Egan, Susannah. 1984. *Patterns of Experience in Autobiography*. Chapel Hill: University of North Carolina Press.

El País. 1977. Editorial. September 15.

Elbaz, Robert. 1988. *The Changing Nature of the Self: A Critical Study of the Autobiographic Discourse*. London: Croom Helm.

Enders, Victoria Lorée, and Pamela Beth Radcliff. 1999. *Constructing Spanish Womanhood: Female Identity in Modern Spain*. Albany: State University of New York Press.

Esdaile, Charles. 2000. *Spain in the Liberal Age: From Constitution to Civil War, 1808–1939*. Oxford: Blackwell.

Estébanez Gil, Juan Carlos. 1995. *María Teresa León: Estudio de su obra literaria*. Burgos: Olmeda.

Eysteinsson, Astradur. 1990. *The Concept of Modernism*. Ithaca: Cornell University Press.

Fagoaga, Concha. 1985. *La voz y el voto de las mujeres: El sufragismo en España, 1877–1931*. Barcelona: Icaria.

Fajardo, Salvador Jiménez, and John C. Wilcox, eds. 1983. *At Home and Beyond: New Essays on Spanish Poets of the Twenties*. Nebraska: Society of Spanish and Spanish-American Studies.

Felman, Shoshana. 1992. The Return of the Voice: Claude Lanzmann's *Shoah*. In Felman and Laub 1992, 204–83.

Felman, Shoshana, and Dori Laub. 1992. *Testimony: Crises of Witnessing in Literature, Psychoanalysis, and History*. New York: Routledge.

Felski, Rita. 1995. *The Gender of Modernity*. Cambridge: Harvard University Press.

Fernández, James D. 1992. *Apology to Apostrophe: Autobiography and the Rhetoric of Self-Representation in Spain*. Durham: Duke University Press.

Ferrán, Ofelia. 2005. *Memoria de la melancolía* by María Teresa León: The Performativity and Disidentification of Exilic Memories. *Journal of Spanish Cultural Studies* 6:59–78.

Fincher, Ruth, and Jane M. Jacobs. 1998. *Cities of Difference*. New York: Guilford.

Flecha García, Consuelo. 1996. *Las primeras universitarias en España, 1872–1910*. Madrid: Narcea.

Folguera, Pilar. 1995. El siglo XX. In *Las mujeres de Madrid como agentes de cambio social*, ed. Margarita Ortega López, 177–236. Madrid: Instituto Universitario de Estudios de la Mujer, Universidad Autónoma de Madrid.

Formica, Mercedes. 1982. *Visto y vivido 1931–1937*. Barcelona: Planeta.

———. 1984. *Escucho el silencio*. Barcelona: Planeta.

———. 1998. *Espejo roto. Y espejuelos*. Madrid: Huerga y Fierro.

Fox, Inman. 1997. *La invención de España: Nacionalismo liberal e identidad nacional.* Madrid: Cátedra.

Freud, Sigmund. 1984. Mourning and Melancholia. In *On Metapsychology: The Theory of Psychoanalysis.* Vol. 11 of *The Pelican Freud Library,* trans. James Strachey, 245–68. Harmondsworth: Penguin.

Gaos, Vicente. 1965. *Antología del grupo poético de 1927.* Salamanca: Anaya.

García Navarro, Pedro de Alcántara. 1885. El problema de la educación de la mujer, sus direcciones principales y datos que deben tenerse en cuenta para resolverlo. *Revista de España* 104:527–50.

Geist, Anthony L., and José B. Monleón, eds. 1999. *Modernism and Its Margins: Reinscribing Cultural Modernity from Spain and Latin America.* New York: Garland.

Geyer, Michael, and Miriam Hansen. 1994. German-Jewish Memory and National Consciousness. In Hartman 1994, 175–90.

Gies, David T., ed. 2004. *The Cambridge History of Spanish Literature.* Cambridge: Cambridge University Press.

Gilmore, Leigh. 1994. The Mark of Autobiography: Postmodernism, Autobiography, and Genre. In *Autobiography and Postmodernism,* ed. Kathleen Ashley, Leigh Gilmore, and Gerald Peters, 3–18. Amherst: University of Massachusetts Press.

Gluck, Sherna Berger, and Daphne Patai, eds. 1991. *Women's Words: The Feminist Practice of Oral History.* New York: Routledge.

González, Ángel. 1976. *El grupo poético de 1927: Antología.* Madrid: Taurus.

Graham, Helen. 1995a. Gender and the State: Women in the 1940s. In Graham and Labanyi 1995, 182–95.

———. 1995b. Women and Social Change. In Graham and Labanyi 1995, 99–116.

Graham, Helen, and Jo Labanyi, eds. 1995. *Spanish Cultural Studies: An Introduction.* Oxford: Oxford University Press.

Gullón, Germán. 1992. *La novela moderna en España (1885–1902): Los albores de la modernidad.* Madrid: Taurus.

Gullón, Ricardo, ed. 1961. *Relaciones amistosas y literarias entre Juan Ramón Jiménez y los Martínez Sierra.* San Juan: Universidad de Puerto Rico.

———. 1969. *La invención del 98 y otros ensayos.* Madrid: Gredos.

———. 1990. *Direcciones del Modernismo.* Madrid: Alianza.

Gusdorf, George. 1980. Conditions and Limits of Autobiography. In Olney 1980, 28–48.

Halbwachs, Maurice. 1992. *On Collective Memory.* Trans. and ed. Lewis A. Coser. Chicago: University of Chicago Press.

Harris, Derek, ed. 1995. *The Spanish Avant-garde.* Manchester: Manchester University Press.

Hartman, Geoffrey H., ed. 1994. *Holocaust Remembrance: The Shapes of Memory.* Oxford: Blackwell.

Heilbrun, Carolyn. 1989. *Writing a Woman's Life.* London: Women's Press.

Henige, David. 1982. *Oral Historiography.* London: Longman.

Hurtado, Amparo. 1998a. Biografía de una generación: Las escritoras del noventa y ocho. In Zavala 1998, 139–54.

———. 1998b. Prologue to Baroja y Nessi 1998, 9–38.

Ibárruri, Dolores. 1984. *Memorias de Pasionaria, 1939–1977: Me faltaba España.* Barcelona: Planeta.

———. 1992. *El único camino.* Madrid: Castalia. (Orig. pub. 1962.)

Infante, José. 1986. *El 27: Retrato de una generación.* Madrid: Club Internacional del Libro.

Ingram, Angela. 1989. On the Contrary, Outside of It. In Broe and Ingram 1989, 1–15.

Jaraiz Franco, Pilar. 1981. *Historia de una disidencia.* Barcelona: Planeta.

Jay, Paul. 1984. *Being in the Text.* Ithaca: Cornell University Press.

Jelinek, Estelle C. 1980a. The Emergence of Women's Autobiography and the Male Tradition. In Jelinek 1980b, 1–20.

———, ed. 1980b. *Women's Autobiography: Essays in Criticism.* Bloomington: Indiana University Press.

Jiménez-Fajardo, Salvador. 1985. *Multiple Spaces: The Poetry of Rafael Alberti.* London: Tamesis.

Johnson, Roberta. 1996. Gender and Nation in Spanish Fiction Between the Wars (1898–1936). *Revista Canadiense de Estudios Hispánicos* 21:167–79.

———. 2003. *Gender and Nation in the Spanish Modernist Novel.* Nashville, TN: Vanderbilt University Press.

Jover Zamora, José María, Guadalupe Gómez-Ferrer Morant, and Juan Pablo Fusi Aizpúrua. 2001. *España: Sociedad, política y civilización (siglos XIX–XX).* Madrid: Debate.

Kaplan, Caren. 1992. Resisting Autobiography: Out-Law Genres and Transnational Feminist Subjects. In Smith and Watson 1992, 115–38.

Kaplan, Temma. 1992. *Red City, Blue Period: Social Movements in Picasso's Barcelona.* Berkeley: University of California Press.

King, Nicola. 2000. *Memory, Narrative, Identity: Remembering the Self.* Edinburgh: Edinburgh University Press.

Kirkpatrick, Susan. 1999. Gender and Modernist Discourse: Emilia Pardo Bazán's *Dulce Dueño.* In Geist and Monleón 1999, 117–39.

———. 2003. *Mujer, modernismo y vanguardia en España (1898–1931).* Trans. Jacqueline Cruz. Madrid: Cátedra.

Lafitte, María. 1964. *La mujer en España: Cien años de su historia.* Madrid: Aguilar.

Laín Entralgo, Pedro. 1945. *Las generaciones en la historia.* Madrid: Instituto de Estudios Políticos.

———. 1970. *La generación del noventa y ocho.* Madrid: Espasa-Calpe. (Orig. pub. 1945.)

Lang, Berel. 1999. *The Future of the Holocaust: Between History and Memory.* Ithaca: Cornell University Press.

Lara Pozuelo, Antonio, ed. 1991. *La autobiografía en lengua española en el siglo XX.* Lausanne: Sociedad Suiza de Estudios Hispánicos.

Leggott, Sarah. 2001. *History and Autobiography in Contemporary Spanish Women's Testimonial Writings.* Lewiston, PA: Mellen.

Lejeune, Philippe. 1989. *On Autobiography.* Ed. Paul John Eakin. Trans. Katherine Leary. Minneapolis: University of Minnesota Press.

León, María Teresa. 1944. *La historia tiene la palabra: Noticia sobre el salvamento del tesoro artístico.* Buenos Aires: Patronato Hispano-Argentino de Cultura.

———. 1958. *Nuestro hogar de cada día: Breviario para la mujer de su casa.* Buenos Aires: Compañía General Fabril.

———. 1987. *Juego limpio.* Barcelona: Seix Barral. (Orig. pub. 1959.)

———. 1998. *Memoria de la melancolía.* Ed. Gregorio Torres Nebrera. Madrid: Castalia. (Orig. pub. 1970.)

Lerner, Gerda. 1976. Placing Women in History: A 1975 Perspective. In *Liberating Women's History: Theoretical and Critical Essays,* ed. Berenice A. Carroll, 357–67. Urbana: University of Illinois Press.

Leydesdorff, Selma, Luisa Passerini, and Paul Thompson, eds. 1996. *Gender and Memory: International Yearbook of Oral History.* Vol. 4. Oxford: Oxford University Press.

Little, Jo, Linda Peake, and Pat Richardson, eds. 1988. *Women in Cities: Gender and the Urban Environment.* Basingstoke: Macmillan.

Lizarraga Vizcarra, Isabel. 2004. *María Lejárraga, Pedagoga: Cuentos breves y otros textos.* Logroño: Instituto de Estudios Riojanos.

Loesberg, Jonathan. 1981. Autobiography as Genre, Act of Consciousness, Text. *Prose Studies* 4:169–85.

López, Helena. 2004. Algunas claves para una lectura feminista de *Memoria de la melancolía,* de María Teresa León. *Journal of Iberian and Latin American Studies* 10:147–67.

Loureiro, Ángel. 1991. La autobiografía española: Actualidad y futuro. *Anthropos* 125:17–20.

———. 2000. *The Ethics of Autobiography: Replacing the Subject in Modern Spain.* Nashville, TN: Vanderbilt University Press.

Lyceum Club Femenino: Reglamento. 1929. Madrid: R. Velasco.

Mainer, José-Carlos. 1983. *La Edad de Plata, 1902–1939.* Madrid: Cátedra.

———. 1989. Las escritoras del 27 (con María Teresa León al fondo). In *Homenaje a María Teresa León,* 13–39. Madrid: Universidad Complutense de Madrid.

Mangini, Shirley. 1995. *Memories of Resistance: Women's Voices from the Spanish Civil War.* New Haven: Yale University Press.

———. 2001. *Las modernas de Madrid: Las grandes intelectuales españolas de la vanguardia.* Barcelona: Península.

Marañón, Gregorio. 1926. *Tres ensayos sobre la vida sexual.* Madrid: Biblioteca Nueva.

Marcus, Laura. 1994. *Auto/biographical Discourses: Theory, Criticism, Practice.* Manchester: Manchester University Press.

Marías, Julián. 1949. *El método histórico de las generaciones.* Madrid: Revista de Occidente.

Martín Gaite, Carmen. 1992. Prologue to *Celia: Lo que dice,* by Elena Fortún, 7–37. Madrid: Alianza.

———. 2004. *Courtship Customs in Postwar Spain (Usos amorosos de la postguerra española).* Trans. Margaret E. W. Jones. Lewisburg, PA: Bucknell.

Martínez Olmedilla, Augusto. 1947. *Los teatros de Madrid: Anecdotario de la farándula madrileña*. Madrid: José Ruiz Alonso.

———. 1961. *Arriba el telón*. Madrid: Aguilar.

Martínez Sierra, Gregorio. 1898. *El poema del trabajo*. Madrid: Eusebio Sánchez.

———. 1911. *Canción de cuna*. Madrid: R. Velasco, 1911.

———. 1916. *Cartas a las mujeres de España*. Madrid: Clásica Española.

———. 1917. *Feminismo, feminidad, españolismo*. Madrid: Renacimiento.

———. 1920. *La mujer moderna*. Madrid: Estrella.

———. 1932. *Nuevas cartas a las mujeres de España*. Madrid: Ibero Americana.

Martínez Sierra, María. 1899. *Cuentos breves: Lecturas recreativas para niños*. Madrid: Enrique Rojas.

———. 1931. *La mujer española ante la república*. Madrid: Esfinge.

———. 1989. *Una mujer por caminos de España*. Ed. Alda Blanco. Madrid: Castalia. (Orig. pub. 1952.)

———. 2000. *Gregorio y yo: Medio siglo de colaboración*. Ed. Alda Blanco. Valencia: Pre-Textos. (Orig. pub. 1953.)

Masanet, Lydia. 1998. *La autobiografía femenina española contemporánea*. Madrid: Fundamentos.

Méndez, Concha. 1926. *Inquietudes: Poemas*. Madrid: Juan Pueyo.

———. 1928. *Surtidor: Poesías*. Madrid: Argis.

———. 1930. *Canciones de mar y tierra*. Buenos Aires: Talleres Gráficos Argentinos.

———. 1990. *Memorias habladas, memorias armadas*. Ed. Paloma Ulacia Altolaguirre. Madrid: Mondadori.

Miller, Tyrus. 1999. *Late Modernism: Politics, Fiction, and the Arts Between the World Wars*. Berkeley: University of California Press.

Miró, Emilio. 2001. *El personaje presentido* de Concha Méndez. In Valender 2001c, 177–91.

Monleón, José. 1977. Evocación del teatro de Arte y Propaganda. *Triunfo*, September 3, 38–40.

Montero, Enrique. 1995. Reform Idealized: The Intellectual and Ideological Origins of the Second Republic. In Graham and Labanyi 1995, 124–33.

Montseny, Federica. 1987. *Mis primeros cuarenta años*. Barcelona: Plaza y Janés.

Mora, Constancia de la. 1939. *In Place of Splendor: The Autobiography of a Spanish Woman*. New York: Harcourt Brace.

Morla Lynch, Carlos. 1958. *En España con Federico García Lorca: Páginas de un diario íntimo, 1928–1936*. Madrid: Aguilar.

Nash, Mary. 1981. *Mujer y movimiento obrero en España*. Barcelona: Fontamara.

———. 1983. *Mujer, familia y trabajo en España, 1875–1936*. Barcelona: Anthropos.

———. 1994. Pronatalism and Motherhood in Franco's Spain. In *Maternity and Gender Policies: Women and the Rise of the European Welfare States, 1880s–1950s*, ed. Gisela Bock and Pat Thane, 160–77. London: Routledge.

———. 1995. *Defying Male Civilization: Women in the Spanish Civil War*. Denver, CO: Arden.

———. 1999. Un/Contested Identities: Motherhood, Sex Reform and the Modernization of Gender Identity in Early Twentieth-Century Spain. In Enders and Radcliff 1999, 25–49.

Neira, Julio, ed. 2004. *Rafael Alberti y María Teresa León cumplen cien años: Encuentro internacional.* Santander: Caja Cantabria.

Nieva de la Paz, Pilar. 1993. *Autoras dramáticas españolas entre 1918 y 1936: Texto y representación.* Madrid: Consejo Superior de Investigaciones Científicas.

———. 1998. Revisando el canon: Hacia una selección crítica del teatro escrito por mujeres en la España de entreguerras. In Zavala 1998, 155–84.

———. 2001. El teatro infantil de Concha Méndez. In Valender 2001c, 165–76.

Nora, Pierre. 1996. *Conflicts and Divisions.* Vol. 1 of *Realms of Memory: Rethinking the French Past.* Trans. Arthur Goldhammer. New York: Columbia University Press.

Núñez Pérez, María Gloria. 1993. *Madrid 1931: Mujeres entre la permanencia y el cambio.* Madrid: Horas y Horas.

Nussbaum, Felicity A. 1989. *The Autobiographical Subject: Gender and Ideology in Eighteenth-Century England.* Baltimore: Johns Hopkins University Press.

O'Connor, Patricia W. 1977. *Gregorio and María Martínez Sierra.* Boston: Twayne.

———. 2000. Los exilios de María Martínez Sierra. In *Sesenta años después: El exilio literario asturiano de 1939,* 277–87. Oviedo: Universidad de Oviedo.

———. 2003. *Mito y realidad de una dramaturga española: María Martínez Sierra.* Logroño: Instituto de Estudios Riojanos.

Olney, James, ed. 1980. *Autobiography: Essays Theoretical and Critical.* Princeton, NJ: Princeton University Press.

———. 1998. *Memory and Narrative: The Weave of Life-Writing.* Chicago: University of Chicago Press.

Oropesa, Salvador. 1997. Estrategias narrativas en *Memoria de la melancolía* de María Teresa León. *Bazar: Revista de Literatura* 4:128–35.

Ortega y Gasset, José. 1963. *Meditaciones del Quijote.* Madrid: Revista de Occidente. (Orig. pub. 1914.)

Pacheco, Bettina. 2001. *Mujer y autobiografía en la España contemporánea.* San Cristóbal, Venezuela: Grupo de Investigación en Literatura Latinoamericana y del Caribe.

Pascal, Roy. 1960. *Design and Truth in Autobiography.* London: Routledge.

Pérez, Janet. 1988–89. Vanguardism, Modernism and Spanish Women Writers in the Years Between the Wars. *Siglo XX/20th Century* 6:40–47.

———. 1996. *Modern and Contemporary Spanish Women Poets.* New York: Twayne.

Pérez Ferrero, Miguel. 1972. *Vida de Pío Baroja.* 2nd ed. Madrid: Magisterio Español.

Petersen, Julius. 1946. Las generaciones literarias. In *Filosofía de la ciencia literaria,* trans. Carlos Silva, 137–93. Mexico City: Fondo de Cultura Económica. (Orig. pub. 1930.)

Pollock, Griselda. 1988. *Vision and Difference: Femininity, Feminism and the Histories of Art.* London: Routledge.

Pompeyo, Gener. 1889. De la mujer y sus derechos en las sociedades modernas. *La Vanguardia,* February 26.

Pope, Randolph. 1974. *La autobiografía española hasta Torres Villarroel.* Vienna: Lang.

Preston, Paul. 1986. *The Spanish Civil War, 1936–1939*. London: Weidenfeld and Nicolson.

Quance, Roberta. 2001. Hacia una mujer nueva. In Valender 2001c, 101–13.

———. 2003. Norah Borges Illustrates Two Spanish Women Poets. In *Crossing Fields in Modern Spanish Culture*, ed. Federico Bonaddio and Xon de Ros, 54–66. Oxford: Legenda.

Quinones, Ricardo J. 1985. *Mapping Literary Modernism: Time and Development*. Princeton, NJ: Princeton University Press.

Ramos, Julio. 1989. *Desencuentros de la modernidad en América Latina: Literatura y política en el siglo XIX*. Mexico City: Fondo de Cultura Económica.

Resina, Joan Ramón. 2000. *Disremembering the Dictatorship: The Politics of Memory in the Spanish Transition to Democracy*. Amsterdam: Rodopi.

Reyero Hermosilla, Carlos. 1980. *Gregorio Martínez Sierra y su teatro del arte*. Madrid: Fundación Juan March.

Richardson, Angelique, and Chris Willis, eds. 2001. *The New Woman in Fiction and in Fact: Fin-de-Siècle Feminisms*. Basingstoke: Palgrave.

Ringrose, David. 1996. *Spain, Europe and the "Spanish Miracle," 1700–1900*. Cambridge: Cambridge University Press.

Rodrigo, Antonina. 1994. *María Lejárraga: Una mujer en la sombra*. Madrid: Vosa.

———. 2002. *Mujeres para la historia: La España silenciada del siglo XX*. Barcelona: Carena.

Rodríguez Puértolas, Julio. 1987. *Literatura fascista española*. Vol. 2. Madrid: Akal.

Roldán, Santiago, and José Luis García Delgado. 1973. *La formación de la sociedad capitalista en España, 1914–1920*. 2 vols. Madrid: Confederación Española de Cajas de Ahorro.

Romero Marín, Juan José. 2000. Lejárraga García, María de la O. In *Mujeres en la historia de España: Enciclopedia biográfica*, ed. Cándida Martínez López and Susanna Tavera, 561–65. Barcelona: Planeta.

Rozas, Juan Manuel. 1978. *El 27 como generación*. Santander: Isla de los Ratones.

Ruiz Guerrero, Cristina. 1997. *Panorama de escritoras españolas*. Vol. 2. Cádiz: Universidad de Cádiz.

Sainz de Robles, Federico Carlos. 1971. *Raros y olvidados*. Madrid: Prensa Española.

Salinas, Pedro. 1941. *Literatura española: Siglo XX*. Mexico City: Séneca.

Salinas, Pedro, and Jorge Guillén. 1992. *Correspondencia: 1923–1951*. Ed. Andrés Soria Olmedo. Barcelona: Tusquets.

Santiáñez, Nil. 2004. Great Masters of Spanish Modernism. In Gies 2004, 479–99.

Scanlon, Geraldine M. 1986. *La polémica feminista en la España contemporánea: 1868–1974*. Trans. Rafael Mazarrasa. Madrid: Akal.

Shubert, Adrian. 1990. *A Social History of Modern Spain*. Winchester, MA: Unwin Hyman.

Sieburth, Stephanie. 1994. *Inventing High and Low: Literature, Mass Culture, and Uneven Modernity in Spain*. Durham: Duke University Press.

Silva, Emilio, and Santiago Macías. 2003. *Las fosas de Franco: Los republicanos que el dictador dejó en las cunetas*. Madrid: Temas de Hoy.

Smith, Barbara Herrnstein. 1984. Contingencies of Value. In Von Hallberg 1984, 5–39.

Smith, Paul. 1988. *Discerning the Subject*. Minneapolis: University of Minnesota Press.

Smith, Sidonie. 1987. *A Poetics of Women's Autobiography: Marginality and the Fictions of Self-Representation*. Bloomington: Indiana University Press.

———. 1993. *Subjectivity, Identity, and the Body: Women's Autobiographical Practices in the Twentieth Century*. Bloomington: Indiana University Press.

———. 2001. *Moving Lives: 20th-Century Women's Travel Writing*. Minneapolis: University of Minnesota Press.

Smith, Sidonie, and Julia Watson, eds. 1992. *De/Colonizing the Subject: The Politics of Gender in Women's Autobiography*. Minneapolis: University of Minnesota Press.

Soufas, C. Christopher Jr. 1989. *Conflict of Light and Wind: The Spanish Generation of 1927 and the Ideology of Poetic Form*. Middletown, CT: Wesleyan University Press.

———. 1991–92. A Relaxed Response to the Review of *Conflict of Light and Wind* by Margaret Persin. *Siglo XX/20th Century* 9:267–69.

———. 1998. Tradition as an Ideological Weapon: The Critical Redefinition of Modernity and Modernism in Early 20th-Century Spanish Literature." *Anales de la literatura española contemporánea* 23:465–77.

Spadaccini, Nicholas, and Jenaro Talens, eds. 1988. *Autobiography in Early Modern Spain*. Minneapolis: Prisma Institute.

Spain, Daphne. 1992. *Gendered Spaces*. Chapel Hill: University of North Carolina Press.

Stanton, Domna C., ed. 1987. *The Female Autograph: Theory and Practice of Autobiography from the Tenth to the Twentieth Century*. Chicago: University of Chicago Press. (Orig. pub. 1984.)

Stewart, Melissa A. 1998. Poet Wives María Teresa León and Anna Murià Tell Their Stories in Alternative Texts. *Letras Peninsulares* 11:223–37.

Suleiman, Susan Rubin. 1990. *Subversive Intent: Gender, Politics, and the Avant-Garde*. Cambridge: Harvard University Press.

Thomas, Hugh. 1989. *The Spanish Civil War*. 4th ed. London: Penguin.

Thompson, Paul. 1988. *The Voice of the Past: Oral History*. 2nd ed. Oxford: Oxford University Press.

Torres Nebrera, Gregorio. 1987. *La obra literaria de María Teresa León: Autobiografía, biografía, novelas*. Cáceres: Universidad de Extremadura.

———. 1996. *Los espacios de la memoria: La obra literaria de María Teresa León*. Madrid: Ediciones de la Torre.

———. 1998. Introduction to León 1998, 7–59.

Tortella, Gabriel. 2000. *The Development of Modern Spain: An Economic History of the Nineteenth and Twentieth Centuries*. Trans. Valerie J. Herr. Cambridge: Harvard University Press.

Tuñón de Lara, Manuel. 1976. *La Segunda República*. Vol. 2. Madrid: Siglo Veintiuno.

Tusell, Javier. 1999. *Arte, historia y política en España (1890–1939)*. Madrid: Biblioteca Nueva.

Ugarte, Michael. 1989. *Shifting Ground: Spanish Civil War Exile Literature*. Durham, NC: Duke University Press.

———. 1994. The Generational Fallacy and Spanish Women Writing in Madrid at the Turn of the Century. *Siglo XX/20th Century* 12:261–76.

———. 1996. *Madrid 1900: The Capital as Cradle of Literature and Culture*. University Park: Pennsylvania State University Press.

Ulacia Altolaguirre, Paloma. 1990. Prologue to Méndez 1990, 15–23.

———. 1993. Concha Méndez y Luis Buñuel. *Ínsula* 553:12–15.

Valender, James. 2001a. Concha Méndez en el Río de la Plata (1929–1930). In Valender 2001c, 149–63.

———, ed. 2001b. *Manuel Altolaguirre y Concha Méndez: Poetas e impresores*. Madrid: Publicaciones de la Residencia de Estudiantes.

———, ed. 2001c. *Una mujer moderna: Concha Méndez en su mundo (1898–1986)*. Madrid: Publicaciones de la Residencia de Estudiantes.

Vásquez, Mary S., ed. 2004. "Besar las sombras": María Teresa León en su centenario, 1903–2003. Special issue, *Letras Peninsulares* 17, no.1.

Vollendorf, Lisa, ed. 2001. *Recovering Spain's Feminist Tradition*. New York: Modern Language Association of America.

Von Hallberg, Robert, ed. 1984. *Canons*. Chicago: University of Chicago Press.

Vosburg, Nancy. 2001. The Tapestry of a Feminist Life: María Teresa León (1903–88). In Vollendorf 2001, 260–77.

Voss, Norine. 1986. "Saying the Unsayable': An Introduction to Women's Autobiography. In *Gender Studies,* ed. Judith Spector, 218–33. Bowling Green, OH: Bowling Green State University Popular Press.

Watson, Martha. 1999. *Lives of Their Own: Rhetorical Dimensions in Autobiographies of Women Activists*. Columbia: University of South Carolina Press.

Wieviorka, Annette. 1994. On Testimony. In Hartman 1994, 23–32.

Wilcox, John C. 1994. Ernestina de Champourcin and Concha Méndez: Their Recision from the Generation of 27. *Siglo XX/20th Century* 12:291–317.

———. 1997. *Women Poets of Spain, 1860–1990: Toward a Gynocentric Vision*. Urbana: University of Illinois Press.

Wilson, Elizabeth. 1991. *The Sphinx in the City: Urban Life, the Control of Disorder, and Women*. Berkeley: University of California Press.

Woolf, Janet. 1993. On the Road Again: Metaphors of Travel in Cultural Criticism. *Cultural Studies* 7:224–39.

Young, James E. 1988. *Writing and Rewriting the Holocaust: Narrative and the Consequences of Interpretation*. Bloomington: Indiana University Press.

———. 1993. *The Texture of Memory: Holocaust Memorials and Meaning*. New Haven: Yale University Press.

Zavala, Iris M., ed. 1998. *La literatura escrita por mujer, desde el siglo XIX hasta la actualidad*. Vol. 5 of *Breve historia feminista de la literatura española (en lengua castellana)*. Barcelona: Anthropos.

Zulueta, Carmen de, and Alicia Moreno. 1993. *Ni convento ni college: La Residencia de Señoritas*. Madrid: Publicaciones de la Residencia de Estudiantes.

Index